ESTATE PLANNING STRATEGIES
For Physicians

Lawrence Farber

**MEDICAL
ECONOMICS
BOOKS**
Oradell, New Jersey 07649

Library of Congress Cataloging in Publication Data

Farber, Lawrence.
  Estate planning strategies for physicians.

  Includes index.
  1. Physicians—Finance, Personal.   2. Estate
planning.   I. Title.   [DNLM: 1. Insurance, Life.
2. Investments.   3. Pensions.   4. Physicians.   5. Wills.
W 79 F219e]
R728.5.F37   1985   332.024'61   85-15236
ISBN 0-87489-256-2

Art Director: Penina Wissner
Design: Jayne Conte

ISBN 0-87489-256-2

Medical Economics Company Inc.
Oradell, New Jersey 07649

Printed in the United States of America

Contents

iv

Publisher's notes

A sound estate plan not only allows you to provide for your family after your death; it can also bring you and your family a number of benefits while you're still alive. *Estate Planning Strategies for Physicians* is designed to help you accomplish both those objectives.

The book carefully takes you through all the necessary steps from preserving the value of your practice and other professional assets to preparing your will. They include the all important tax- and expense-saving strategies and tips involving insurance, investments, gifts, and pension funds. And it helps you find and use the best advisers, trustees, and executor. Whether you're married or single, in private or corporate practice, this book gives you the guidelines you need to set up, secure, and build your estate.

Lawrence Farber is a senior editor of *Medical Economics* magazine, and a member of its editorial board. He has written and edited hundreds of articles on all aspects of medical practice and financial management. He is the author of *Tax Strategy for Physicians, 3rd Edition,* and *Personal Money Management for Physicians, 3rd Edition,* and is the editor of *Medical Economics Encyclopedia of Practice and Financial Management,* all published by Medical Economics Books.

Acknowledgment

Grateful acknowledgment is made to attorney Bernard H. Greene for guidance in the preparation of this book. Mr. Greene, for a number of years a visiting lecturer on estate planning at Yale Law School, is a member of the New York law firm of Paul, Weiss, Rifkind, Wharton & Garrison.

1

Plan for yourself as well as your heirs

Your estate plan should be a great deal more concerned with life than with death. Granted, mortality is a factor you must consider, but the odds are that you and those you care about will have many years to benefit from the fruits of your labors. Maximizing those benefits and distributing them where they'll do the most good is what estate planning is all about.

Taxes are an obvious threat to diminish the size of your estate, and your plan should include measures to de-fang the government wolves. At the same time, however, you don't want to concentrate so single-mindedly on tax avoidance that you needlessly restrict what you and your heirs can do with your money. Happily, the income and estate tax laws have been liberalized in recent years, making it easier than before to dispose of your assets as you wish. On the other hand, your ultimate estate is likely to be larger than you formerly thought it would be, so you can't blithely ignore possible federal and state taxes. Chapter 2 puts the tax dangers in perspective and explains how to shield your spouse, children, and grandchildren from them when necessary.

Writing a proper will is important to the success of your estate plan. You may already have a will, but like any document that's expected to be in force a long time and cover a variety of contingencies, it requires adjustment to changed circumstances. A doctor's first will is often drawn up while still in training. Typically, it leaves everything to his spouse and names his parents as secondary beneficiaries. In too many cases, that first will is still in effect when the doctor dies years later, leaving a much bigger estate and children of different ages. The doctor's parents may be in need; the executor may be unable to serve; a sizable estate tax liability may loom. Yet the will still reads the way it did when the doctor was a resident. (Appendix 1 is a will-review checklist.)

Among the questions to consider in writing your will—covered in Chapter 3—is whether it's desirable to set up a trust for your spouse; at what ages your children should receive their inheritances; whether a child requires special treatment; how to provide for grandchildren, parents, other deserving relatives, friends, and charities.

If your children are young, your will should name guardians for them in case you and your spouse both die while they're still minors. Careful thought must be given to choosing guardians who can fulfill these responsibilities. Chapter 3 discusses this in detail, along with such matters as providing for the offspring of an earlier marriage and guarding against a will contest.

However precise and astute your planning, others besides you will eventually have to carry it out. Chapter 4 suggests steps you can take to make the administration of your estate as easy and economical as possible; to select executors and trustees who are not only competent in business affairs but also attuned to the needs and desires of your beneficiaries; to lessen probate costs and delays; and to assure sufficient cash to pay taxes and family expenses.

Many of your planning decisions will logically depend on the type and amount of assets you own. During the course of your career, the size and character of your holdings are bound to change. In the early stages, you'll very likely have to look to life insurance to provide an instant estate as protection for your family if you die prematurely. And you'll probably rely on disability coverage to guard against interruption of earnings by illness or injury. As time goes by and your nest egg grows, insurance may play a less vital role but still be useful as a source of funds in retirement or to meet estate expenses. Chapter 5 describes and evaluates the various types of policies and annuities being offered, including some recent innovations. It shows how to match coverage to changing needs; how to select policies to be dropped when that becomes appropriate; and how to prevent estate and income taxes from eroding the benefits of insurance for yourself and your heirs.

Few elements in doctors' financial programs merit greater attention than tax-sheltered pension funds. In many cases, especially for a physician under 50, the money in the fund will reach the high six figures or more if the right kind of plan is chosen and contributions are made to the legal limit. If you die before retirement, the fund will constitute a substantial legacy for your spouse or other beneficiary. With so much money potentially at stake, payout methods and tax implications need careful consideration. To achieve the greatest advantages from your retirement program, you should be certain that it dovetails with your life insurance and other aspects of your estate plan. Chapter 6 covers these points in detail.

How large an estate you can build for yourself and your family rests not only on the amount of money you put into savings but also on your skill in investing it. While recommending specific investments is beyond the scope of this book, Chapter 7 weighs the considerations involved in selecting growth and income securities and real estate for doctors' portfolios, both pension and nonpension. Also discussed are ways you can help alleviate problems your heirs may face when they inherit your investments.

If your practice is incorporated, you have opportunities to build extra flexibility into your estate plan and improve the benefits of your retirement and insurance programs. Also, nonmedical corporations and trust-leaseback arrangements offer income and estate tax advantages, as outlined in Chapter 8.

Whether you're incorporated or not, you'll want to make sure that you or your heirs receive the full value of your share of the practice assets when you depart. A carefully drawn buy-sell agreement with your associates is the recommended method for accomplishing that in a multidoctor practice. Chapter 9 spells out the provisions the agreement should contain and also describes the steps a solo physician can take to realize his practice's worth.

As your assets grow with the years, you may become able to afford sizable lifetime gifts that confer a double benefit. They offer the satisfaction of helping your heirs now, when they need it most. In addition, those gifts may save you and your heirs taxes, if made the right way. Chapter 10 compares the advantages and drawbacks of different custodial and trust arrangements for gifts to minors. It also shows how you can obtain large tax savings by removing assets with growth potential from your future taxable estate. And it suggests methods of donating to charity that can reduce income tax in your lifetime and estate tax after death.

The typical doctor is married, and this assumption is implicit in the foregoing chapters. Many of the observations and suggestions offered apply equally well even if you're single, divorced, or widowed. But your estate tax exposure is much greater when you're single, and, of course, the absence of a spouse will affect your planning in other ways. Chapter 11 deals with these special problems, as well as with the economic and tax effects of a divorce on your estate plan.

Here it's appropriate to say that estate planning is, in principle, gender-free. To reflect this, the neutral word "spouse" is frequently used in the chapters that follow. Yet in some contexts it's more suitable to bow to statistical reality by referring to the doctor as "he" and to the spouse as "his wife."

A final point to be stressed: The basic estate-planning decisions are yours to make, but you'll need the assistance of an attorney and other competent advisers to shape your plan in accordance with your goals. This book is not intended to take the place of such counsel, but it can help you get the most from the experts you hire. Guidelines for selecting them are in Chapter 12.

There's no denying that estate planning, done thoroughly, will cost you time and money. If you have lingering doubts that they'll be well spent, these vignettes from a Medical Economics survey of doctors' widows may help to convince you:

☐ After a 58-year-old East Coast neurosurgeon died in an accident, a vaguely worded buy-and-sell agreement forced the widow to sue his partner for $60,000 he refused to pay her. She was awarded $40,000, of which

$15,000 went to her lawyer. Payments for her husband's final monthly salary and accrued vacation time were never made.

☐ At age 34, a New Mexico internist came down with Hodgkins disease. He was out of work for only six months after surgery, but the disability insurance payments fell far short of his lost income. They ceased altogether when the doctor returned to practice, even though his condition limited his hours, and he had to borrow from a bank and his pension plan to pay office salaries. When he died two years later, his widow had to sell the house and take a job while caring for their young child.

☐ A Southern radiologist's will set up a trust for his wife and children. Though she was financially knowledgeable, a bank was named sole trustee in the will, prepared by the bank's law firm. The bank refused to allow the widow funds to continue payments on an investment property, which had to be sold at a loss. Amounts allocated in the trust document for the children's education were much less than current tuition charges, but the bank raised them only under threat of a lawsuit.

☐ A Maryland pediatrician left no instructions to his widow about disposing of his practice. She simply turned it over to another physician for free. Another widow was unable to collect $100,000 in accounts receivable. Others were forced to sell equipment and furnishings at a fraction of their value.

Could such things happen if you fell sick or died unexpectedly? Then it's time to get cracking.

2

Take the sting out of taxes

Taxes are a key element in estate planning. Failure to take them into account can cost a doctor's heirs thousands—sometimes hundreds of thousands—of dollars. On the other hand, maneuvers to avoid taxes may complicate your plan, increase its cost, and place undesirable restrictions on your own or your family's freedom to make use of your assets. So it's important to determine how necessary any tax-saving measures are before you undertake them.

A logical way to begin is by estimating your present net worth (see Box 2A). This figure is not the same as your taxable estate, but it will do for the purpose of sizing up the potential tax problem. If your net worth—what you own less what you owe—isn't more than $600,000, all of it can go right to your heirs free of any federal estate tax. That's the exemption available to every estate.

If your estate is larger than the exemption, the excess is taxable at a rate starting at 37 percent and progressing up to 55 percent. However, any amount you bequeath to your spouse—whether $10 or $10 million—escapes tax at your death. But that's only a temporary respite if your spouse leaves more than $600,000 when she dies.

Before going further, we need to add these qualifications to the preceding statements:

☐ For tax purposes, proceeds of insurance on your life count as part of your estate if you own the policies. Thus, the estate of a doctor worth, say, $400,000 and insured for another $400,000 would be taxed as if it totaled $800,000. Ways of eliminating insurance from your estate are discussed in Chapter 5.

5

BOX 2A
How much are you worth today?

Use this worksheet to estimate where you stand now. The table in Box 2D shows how many years it may take for your net worth to pass the critical $600,000 tax-free-estate mark, if it's not beyond it already.

Assets

Cash in banks, money funds, etc. $ _____

Retirement-plan share   _____

Market value of home(s)   _____

Market value of investment real estate   _____

Market value of stocks and bonds   _____

Value of collections (art, etc.)   _____

Sideline business (resale value)   _____

Value of other investments   _____

Life insurance cash value   _____

Home furnishings, cars, jewelry, etc.   _____

Debts owed to you, miscellaneous   _____

    Total assets $ _____

Liabilities

Balances outstanding on mortgages
  and other loans $ _____

Taxes payable   _____

Bills due, miscellaneous   _____

    Total liabilities $ _____

Net worth (assets minus liabilities) $ _____

☐ Your taxable estate may also include certain kinds of gifts made during your lifetime. This is explained in detail in Chapter 10. (For a worksheet to help you estimate your taxable estate, see Box 2B.)

☐ The $600,000 exemption applies if death occurs after 1986. This is an increase from $400,000 in 1985 and $500,000 in 1986. Technically, the tax-free amount is due to a credit, not an exemption. (The difference can be significant dollarwise, as explained in Box 2C.)

ANTICIPATING ESTATE GROWTH

According to a recent Medical Economics survey, more than half of all doctors have a net worth under $600,000. If you're one of them, your estate could go tax-free to your heirs, whoever they might be—provided you die in the near future. But chances are you'll live to see your net worth expand considerably (see Box 2D). Some 20 percent of doctors 50 and over are already millionaires, and MDs in their 30s and 40s typically anticipate retiring with $1.5 million or more.

Even if your own projections aren't that rosy, don't be too quick to discount the tax threat. Dr. Arnold, for example, has a wife and two children. Mrs. Arnold has no funds of her own, and the doctor's will leaves her his whole estate—currently less than $600,000. If he died next year, her inheritance would be tax-free, and the estate she'd pass on to the children at her death could well be below $600,000, so they also would get it tax-free.

But what if Arnold's estate grows to, say, $800,000 by the time he dies? The income from that might be enough to support the family, so the children would stand to inherit the entire $800,000 principal from Mrs. Arnold. That would cost them $75,000 in estate tax.

Dr. Arnold can save his children taxes by altering his will to take into account the future growth of his estate. He can, for instance, leave his wife $600,000, with anything over that going to the children. At his death, the marital deduction will shield Mrs. Arnold's portion from tax, and the tax credit will do the same for the children's legacy. When Mrs. Arnold dies, her estate will also be entitled to a credit. So the children will benefit from two credits instead of one. By splitting his estate in this way, Arnold can pass along as much as $1.2 million to his children tax-free.

It may seem that this arrangement saves taxes for your children at the expense of your spouse by limiting her share of your estate. To escape that dilemma, you can leave the children's portion in trust for them, while giving your spouse the right to use the income from that trust as long as she lives. The trustee can even be instructed to dip into principal for your spouse's benefit if that should become necessary. The $600,000 exemption applies to the children's trust at your death. After your spouse dies, the trust fund would go to your children without being subject to any estate tax, since it would not be part of her estate.

BOX 2B
How your estate will be taxed

The principle underlying the estate tax law is that your estate will be taxed as a whole, whether your beneficiaries get it all at your death or you give them part of it during your lifetime. In general, this is how your executor will figure the tax:

First, he'll calculate your "gross estate." In many cases, this is the same as your net worth, except that it includes the **face value** (rather than the cash value) of your life insurance if you own the policies. But the gross estate may also include the value of other items that you might not think of as belonging to you. Some examples: custodial bank accounts where you're the custodian (see Chapter 10); survivor's benefits from annuities you're now receiving; co-owner's shares of jointly held property (see Chapter 11); assets in a revocable trust (see Chapter 4). Valuation is generally based on the fair market value of the estate assets at the date of death, but a date six months later can be used by the executor if that would decrease the value of the gross estate and the estate tax due.

From the gross figure, the executor will subtract final expenses, administrative costs, and other debts not already taken into account. The result is your "adjusted gross estate."

Next, he'll deduct the amount your spouse receives and any legacies to charity. The balance is your "taxable estate." That figure must be increased by the value of any taxable gifts you've made since 1976.

Using the unified gift and estate tax rate schedule (see Box 2C), he'll figure the tentative tax. The reason it's "tentative" is that he then subtracts the gift/estate tax credit which every estate is entitled to. Taxes you actually paid on lifetime gifts since 1976 also count as a credit against the estate tax.

In the case of a married couple, there need be no tax on the estate of the first to die, since the marital deduction is unlimited. But the survivor's estate may be taxed if it's larger than the amount covered by the credit. In the example here, the survivor dies in 1987, leaving an adjusted gross estate of $800,000, with $10,000 of that going to charity. The survivor also made taxable lifetime gifts totaling $60,000 but didn't pay any gift tax while alive because the total "tax" came to less than the credit.

Bear in mind that only **taxable** gifts must be added back into your estate. This means you can save tax by taking advantage of the annual exclusion (see Chapter 10).

8

	Sample figures	Your estimated figures
A. Adjusted gross estate	$800,000	$ _____
B. Amount left to spouse	0	_____
C. Amount left to charity	10,000	_____
D. Total deductions (B plus C)	10,000	_____
E. Taxable estate (A minus D)	790,000	_____
F. Lifetime taxable gifts	60,000	_____
G. Taxable amount (E plus F)	850,000	_____
H. Tentative tax (see Box 2C)	287,300	_____
I. Estate tax credit	192,800	_____
J. Credit for gift tax paid	0	_____
K. Total credits (I plus J)	192,800	_____
L. Tax due (H minus K)	$94,500	$ _____

BOX 2C
Unified gift and estate tax rates

After calculating the tentative tax based on the rates shown, determine the actual tax by subtracting the allowable credit. The maximum credit, $192,800, eliminates tax on estates of $600,000 or less. However, you aren't permitted to treat the $600,000 as an exemption. For example, if the taxable amount is $750,000, you can't subtract $600,000 and figure the tax on $150,000 (which would be $38,800). Instead, you first take the whole $750,000, find the tentative tax ($248,300), and then deduct the $192,800 credit, leaving an actual tax of $55,500.

Taxable amount[1]	Tentative tax[2]	Tax on each additional $1,000
$ 10,000	$ 1,800	$200
20,000	3,800	220
40,000	8,200	240
60,000	13,000	260
80,000	18,200	280
100,000	23,800	300
150,000	38,800	320
250,000	70,800	340
500,000	155,800	370
750,000	248,300	390
1,000,000	345,800	410
1,250,000	448,300	430
1,500,000	555,800	450
2,000,000	780,300	490
2,500,000	1,025,800	500[3]
3,000,000	1,290,800	500[4]

[1] After deductions and adjustments.
[2] Before tax credit; amount of credit depends on year of death: 1985—$121,800, 1986— $155,800, 1987 and thereafter—$192,800.
[3] Effective in 1988 ($530 prior).
[4] $550 prior to 1988.

Some doctors shy away from trusts because they're concerned about the legal entanglements and extra expense. But these objections may be far outweighed by potential tax savings (see Box 2E), as well as by other advantages described in Chapter 3. Ways of minimizing the drawbacks of trusts are detailed in Chapter 4.

SHARING BETWEEN SPOUSE AND CHILDREN

There's more than one way of dividing an estate between spouse and children to minimize taxes. For example, your will could provide that your children (or their trust) receive the maximum amount covered by the tax exemption, with your wife getting the rest. But that formula might not work out as you'd like.

BOX 2D
How long before your estate becomes taxable?

If you die after 1986, you can leave up to $600,000 free of estate tax, even if it doesn't go to your spouse. This table shows how soon your current estate's growth may boost it above that maximum exclusion and make it vulnerable to tax.

Current estate	Number of years to reach $600,000 if annual growth rate is:			
	8%	10%	12%	14%
$200,000	14	12	10	8
250,000	11	9	8	7
300,000	9	7	6	5
350,000	7	6	5	4
400,000	5	4	4	3
450,000	4	3	3	2
500,000	2	2	2	1

Suppose you die after 1986, leaving an estate of $900,000. Then the formula would give your children $600,000 and your wife only $300,000.

A formula leaving your spouse the maximum exempt amount and your children the balance might yield a better result in this case, but not in others. What if your $900,000 estate includes a $200,000 life insurance policy with your wife as beneficiary? The policy proceeds will come to her outside the will (they're not part of the "probate estate"), and the will gives her $600,000, so she winds up with $800,000.

The situation becomes even more complicated if your spouse has or later acquires sizable assets of her own. Then her legacy from you, on top of what she owns, could inflate the tax bill on her estate.

Clearly, you can't be sure what your financial circumstances will be at your death—and therefore how best to split your estate between your spouse and other heirs. You could, of course, keep adjusting the figures by revising your will frequently, but some estate planners suggest a less cumbersome solution: Let your spouse make the adjustment after your death.

For example, a doctor could leave his wife the entire estate except for, say, $100,000 in trust for the children. If he died with a $900,000 estate, she would then be entitled to $800,000. But she could "disclaim" $200,000 of her legacy (or any amount she wished), thereby insuring that *her* estate wouldn't be taxed. The disclaimed amount would add to the doctor's taxable estate, but the credit would cover it.

Your will should stipulate that the entire amount your spouse disclaims is to go into the children's trust. Otherwise, state law might direct some of the disclaimed portion elsewhere. If you want your spouse to get all the income from the children's trust, it's wise to specify in your will that this includes

BOX 2E
Trusts and tax savings

When you set up a trust, you arrange to transfer assets to a trustee and tell him when and to whom he is to distribute income and principal. A trust created by your will is called a "testamentary trust," as distinguished from a "living trust" established in your lifetime.

A living trust may be either "irrevocable"—you give up your power over the assets permanently—or "revocable," in which case you can change the terms or dissolve the trust as you please. A testamentary trust is irrevocable once you're dead, but since it doesn't come into existence until then, you can modify or eliminate it merely by altering your will, so you needn't fear being locked into an unsuitable arrangement if your family or financial circumstances should change. Assets you place in an irrevocable living trust are subject to gift taxes; those you put into a revocable trust are not, unless you later make it irrevocable or give trust assets to someone besides yourself.

One of the main virtues of a trust is its flexibility. For instance, you can instruct the trustee to pay income and/or principal to a beneficiary for life or some shorter specified period, and then distribute what's left—called the "remainder"—to someone else. As explained elsewhere, this can produce gift or estate tax savings.

Trusts can often save income taxes as well. One way is for the trustee to distribute income from trust assets to a beneficiary in a lower tax bracket than yours. That's the rationale behind so-called short-term trusts, discussed in Chapter 10. Income accumulated by an irrevocable trust is taxable to it rather than being piled on top of your own income as would be the case if you still owned the assets. However, when the accumulated income is eventually distributed, the tax must be refigured by the beneficiary as if he had received it in prior years. If the refigured tax is more than the trust paid on the income, the beneficiary owes the difference. This "throwback rule" doesn't normally apply to trust income accumulated for a beneficiary prior to age 21, or to profits from the sale of assets by the trust on which it paid capital-gains tax.

---

income from any disclaimed funds as well. Make certain, too, that your spouse understands the advantages of the right to disclaim and will get proper guidance in exercising it.

If you prefer to have your executor, rather than your spouse, determine the split, your will can instruct him to do so by means of a so-called Q-TIP trust (see Chapter 3). In the preceding example, if the entire $900,000 were left in trust, the executor could claim the marital deduction for the appropriate amount—$600,000 or less. Then only that much would be part of the spouse's estate.

SPLITTING A LARGE ESTATE

If a doctor's taxable estate is larger than $1.2 million, there will be a tax to pay either at his death, his wife's, or both, since their two $600,000 exemptions won't shield all of it. Take a man with a $2-million estate. He can leave

Estate planning strategies for physicians

$600,000 to his children and $1.4 million to his wife free of tax at his death. Assuming she passes her share intact to the children, they'll pay $320,000 in tax when she dies. By splitting his estate evenly between wife and kids, the doctor could shift $400,000 from her top two estate tax brackets to a lower bracket. At his death, there would be a tax of $153,000 on the children's $1 million. When the wife died, her $1-million estate would be taxed the same amount. So the taxes on the two estates would total only $306,000—a saving of $14,000. If the doctor's estate were $5 million instead of $2 million, dividing it equally would save $117,000 for the children.

It's highly questionable whether the potential tax saving is large enough to justify a 50-50 split in ordinary circumstances. First, it involves denying your spouse full control over a sizable chunk of money. Second, it means paying a substantial estate tax when you die instead of deferring it until your spouse dies. If that money *didn't* go to the government at your death, the income from it could, over the years, exceed the potential estate tax saving. However, leaving your spouse less than the maximum may make sense if she's not likely to outlive you by more than a few years, if you prefer to limit the amount she can dispose of freely, or if the estate is rich in assets with high potential for appreciation.

NONMARITAL BEQUESTS THAT SPRING A TAX TRAP

Although federal law supposedly lets you leave an unlimited amount to your spouse tax-free, a carelessly drawn will can stick her with a sizable tax bill just the same. That happened to the wife of a Florida doctor who died a few years ago. His will included bequests of $10,000 apiece to half a dozen relatives other than his wife and children. His wife approved of those bequests, but they cost her a whopping $30,150 in taxes. With proper planning, neither she nor the relatives would have paid any federal estate tax at all.

The doctor's will left his relatives $60,000, his children the maximum amount covered by the tax credit, and his wife the residue of his estate. The federal estate tax on nonmarital bequests—everything not going to the wife—was $19,900. Since the will didn't say anything about payment of estate taxes, state law decided who got the bill.

In some states, the taxes (federal and state, if any) are automatically apportioned among all the heirs according to their shares of the estate. In others, like Florida, the bill goes to the residuary heir—in this case, the wife. So the $19,900 federal tax on the nonmarital bequests had to come from her share, despite the "unlimited" marital deduction. But that wasn't the worst of it. The $19,900 itself was also taxable because of a well-established rule that the marital deduction doesn't exempt any money used to pay estate taxes. This quirk in the law, called "tax on tax," made the wife pay an additional $10,250 in federal taxes, for a total of $30,150.

The doctor's will could have stipulated that his six relatives bear the taxes equally. Then $3,317—one-sixth of $19,900—would have been subtracted from each $10,000 bequest, and his wife wouldn't have owed any tax.

But he could have avoided *all* tax liability for his heirs. How? By leaving the relatives out of his will and letting the wife bestow the gifts after he died. The extra $60,000 she'd inherit would be tax-free to her; so would the six $10,000 gifts she'd make, since the annual gift-tax exclusion (see Chapter 10) would cover them.

This method of saving estate taxes on your nonmarital bequests won't work if you obligate your spouse to make the gifts, by your will or otherwise. In that case, the gift amounts wouldn't be shielded by the marital deduction. So you have to rely on your spouse to carry out your wishes voluntarily after you're gone.

Charitable bequests aren't subject to estate tax and therefore don't create a problem for your spouse. However, there's an advantage to having her make postmortem donations in your name instead of providing for them in your will. If the money goes through your spouse's hands first, she can claim an income tax deduction for the contribution, and it doesn't cost her any estate tax.

WAYS TO CUT STATE INHERITANCE TAXES

In the past, many estate plans concentrated on minimizing federal taxes and virtually ignored state death taxes. These were generally much smaller than the federal tax and could also be used as a credit against it (see Box 2F). But the impact of state death taxes may be greater now.

For example, suppose your will leaves $300,000 to your two minor children and the rest of your estate to your wife. There won't be any federal tax on your estate, but if you're an Indiana resident, the state will collect a tax of $6,900. None of that can be used to trim the federal estate tax since it's down to zero already.

Depending on local law, a similar will may be subject to a state tax varying from zero to several times the Indiana figure. So it makes sense to have your adviser estimate the state tax cost of your present will. If it's sizable, look for tax-saving moves that won't disrupt your plans for your assets or increase the total federal bite.

Most states tax a spouse's inheritance more lightly than other heirs', or even exempt it entirely. (See Appendix 2.) By enlarging your spouse's share, you stand to save on state tax, with no immediate cost in federal tax because of the unlimited marital deduction. However, if your spouse's share is already substantial, adding to it might be undesirable because of the increased tax at *her* death. Remember, she can leave up to $600,000 free of federal tax, but the US will take at least 37 percent of anything above that.

BOX 2F
Credit for state death taxes paid

If your estate or heirs pay state death taxes, a credit for some or all of the amount may be deducted from the federal estate tax owed. The maximum credit is shown in the table. However, the credit claimed can't be larger than the state taxes paid. Many states levy an estate tax exactly equal to the credit (see Appendix 2). This gives them a cut of the federal tax at no cost to your heirs. Example: On a $550,000 taxable estate, a $12,000 credit can be claimed for state taxes paid.

Taxable estate*	Credit	Credit on each additional $10,000 of estate
$ 100,000	$ 0	$ 80
150,000	400	160
200,000	1,200	240
300,000	3,600	320
500,000	10,000	400
700,000	18,000	480
900,000	27,600	560
1,100,000	38,800	640
1,600,000	70,800	720
2,100,000	106,800	800
2,600,000	146,800	880
3,100,000	190,800	960
3,600,000	238,800	1,040
4,100,000	290,800	1,120
5,100,000	402,800	1,200
6,100,000	522,800	1,280
7,100,000	650,800	1,360
8,100,000	786,800	1,440
9,100,000	930,800	1,520
10,100,000	1,082,800	1,600

*Gross estate less all deductions, but not including lifetime gifts.

So you may need a better solution to your state tax problem. If your state treats certain kinds of assets more leniently than others, you may be able to save your heirs money by taking advantage of that fact. For instance, the majority of states exempt from inheritance taxes some or all of the life insurance proceeds that are payable to individuals rather than to the estate. Suppose your wife is now the beneficiary of a $200,000 policy on your life and you plan to leave your adult children assets worth that much. If your state doesn't tax a spouse's inheritance, consider naming the children beneficiaries of the policy, and leaving your wife the assets instead. That won't cost her anything, and the children will get the $200,000 tax-free. The switch won't affect the federal tax.

What if insurance proceeds are subject to inheritance taxes in your state? You may still be able to save your beneficiaries tax by making them the owners of the policies. If you give up all your ownership rights, the proceeds generally won't count as part of your estate for either state or federal tax purposes, though there may be a gift tax.

Estate planners often recommend an insurance trust as the best way to do this, especially when the beneficiaries are minors. Giving your policies to a trust while you live may be desirable even if you want the insurance money to go to your spouse. The trust might not save taxes at *your* death, but it would keep the proceeds out of your spouse's estate. Chapter 5 discusses life insurance trusts in detail.

Consider taking advantage of exemptions for children if you live in a state that totally exempts bequests to your spouse. That way, you can double the amount that the two of you can pass to your children free of state inheritance taxes. For example, Michigan exempts bequests of $10,000 per child, although any amount can pass tax-free to the spouse. A Michigan physician with three children could will them each $10,000, which would be state tax-free at his death. Assuming that his wife also left the children at least $10,000 each, a total of $60,000—$30,000 at each death—can be kept safe from state inheritance taxes.

You may not be able to shield your estate from state taxes altogether. But your will can still shift the burden from your spouse to your other heirs. Because any part of your spouse's inheritance used to pay taxes automatically becomes subject to federal estate tax, relieving her of state tax liability may save federal tax as well.

SAVING ESTATE TAXES FOR YOUR GRANDCHILDREN

As discussed earlier, a standard bypass trust—income to spouse for life, then principal to children—avoids a second estate tax when your spouse dies. But the children's legacies will be taxed again in *their* estates, diminishing your grandchildren's inheritance from you. To prevent this, you can bypass your children as well, in several ways:

☐ Make outright bequests to your *grandchildren* (via custodial accounts, if under age).

☐ Leave the principal in trust for the grandchildren, with the income going to your spouse for life or to them.

☐ Leave the principal in trust for the grandchildren, with your *children* getting the income for life after your spouse dies (or after you do, if she doesn't need the income or dies before you).

With either of the first two alternatives, none of the trust principal will be subject to a second estate tax when your spouse or children die. If you choose the third alternative, however, the trust principal will be taxable as part of your children's estates even though it never passes through their hands. This is known as the "generation-skipping transfer tax." It applies when a trust pays income to someone from a generation younger than yours (e.g., to *your* children), and then pays the principal to someone from a third generation (e.g., to *their* children).

Fortunately, each of your children's estates can claim a $250,000 exemption from this tax. Thus, a doctor who has three children, each with one or more children of their own, can put as much as $750,000 into generation-skipping trusts for his grandchildren, and none of the principal will be taxed to his children's estates. (The number of grandchildren makes no difference, and neither does the number of trusts; only one exemption is permitted for each *child's* estate.)

The answers to the following questions may help you decide whether a generation-skipping trust is appropriate for your family:

Will the trust hurt your children?

They may be self-sufficient now, but unforeseen events—business setbacks, serious health problems—could affect their financial positions. The trust can be written so that the trustee is allowed to distribute part of the principal to your children if they need it.

Will your child's estate be big enough?

Remember that a generation-skipping transfer won't save *your* estate a penny in taxes; it's your child's estate that will get a tax break. But will it be needed? Look at the case of an Oregon neurosurgeon. His older son followed in his footsteps and was earning a six-figure income at age 40. The younger one, however, opted for the academic life at a local college, where his rewards were mostly intellectual. The generation-skipping transfer wouldn't be apt to benefit his children, because his estate is unlikely to exceed $600,000. So the father set up a trust for the older son but left the younger an outright bequest.

Are there nontax considerations?

Aside from tax savings, there are other arguments for a generation-skipping trust. For instance, you may not think very highly of your children's ability to manage money for their children. Or you may want to keep your children from leaving your money to somebody you don't care for. In short, a generation-skipping trust is worth a look for a doctor who has accumulated a sizable estate and would like an extra measure of control over its disbursement. But bear in mind that family harmony is important, too. A trust that isn't acceptable to some of the family members affected can mean a legacy of ill will and legal wrangling. That isn't worth the tax benefit.

3

What to cover in your will

"We want to leave everything to each other. And after we're gone, it should all go to our children." That's practically the theme song for the well-meaning doctors and their spouses who go to have wills drawn. But when their lawyers question these couples more closely, problems inevitably turn up. Maybe one of the children is still under age. Would he know how to handle, say, $200,000 at age 18? Maybe one child has a problem with drugs or has joined a religious cult. Do you really want your money to finance that kind of lifestyle? Maybe you have an elderly parent. Are you sure that if both you and your spouse were out of the picture, that parent would be well cared for?

QUESTIONS YOUR WILL SHOULD ANSWER

There are ways to handle family problems like these. And because almost every family has them, how much you leave after taxes and expenses isn't the only important part of estate planning. It's every bit as important to decide who your heirs really are, how you want them to get their share of your estate, and when. Let's take a look at the people in your life and the questions you have to consider when you're deciding who gets what, as well as the legal formalities your will must follow (see Box 3A).

Should you provide a trust for your spouse?

A trust for your children can save them estate tax as explained in Chapter 2, but what you leave your spouse goes to her tax-free, even if she gets it outright. However, if her legacy is substantial, putting it in trust may have advantages. Possibly your spouse may not want or not be up to managing her own money, or she may need protection from pressure or influence.

Such a "marital" trust—i.e., one that qualifies for the marital deduction—may also have economic benefits. By appointing the same trustee for both the marital and the children's trusts, you'd assure unified management of your estate and avoid any problems that split ownership of your assets might otherwise engender. In addition, a two-trust setup may save your spouse income taxes during her lifetime and estate taxes at her death. Here's how:

Instead of using income from both trusts for your wife's expenses, the trustee could be instructed to pay her what she needs from the income and principal of her trust (call it Trust A), letting the children's trust (Trust B) accumulate income. That way she would be taxed only on the income from Trust A. Trust B would have to pay taxes on its income, but at a lower rate than your wife would pay if she received all the income from both trusts. The money she got from Trust A principal wouldn't be subject to income tax. And over the years, her future taxable estate (what's left of Trust A when she dies) would decline.

If Trust A was exhausted while she was still alive, the trustee would be directed to support her with income and, if necessary, principal from Trust B. Meanwhile, B would grow through its accumulation of income. At your wife's death, whatever was in the trust would go to the children free of estate tax, though there might be some additional income tax then (see throwback rule, Box 2E). Or you can achieve virtually the same tax savings by leaving your spouse's share outright instead of in a marital trust, if she's willing to spend her capital rather than the income from the children's trust. A trustee may be more diligent in pursuing tax savings, but if you adopt the two-trust plan, be sure your trustee understands and agrees that the well-being of your wife and children takes precedence over tax considerations. (For more on the subject of trustees, see Chapter 4.)

When should your children inherit?

You need to deal with this question even if the children won't get anything until your spouse dies, since you don't know when that might happen. Under most states' laws, a child can't take control of an inheritance until he's 18. For younger children, the courts will appoint a guardian to look after the money—usually under strict judicial supervision—if no other provisions have been made. But once a child reaches 18, he gets it all—unless the will specifies otherwise.

If you're like most parents, you probably feel that an 18-year-old—no matter how mature and responsible—isn't ready to deal with a sizable amount of money. Maybe the right time will be when he's 21 or when he gets out of college. You might want to delay the inheritance until age 25 or later, to allow time for graduate study or a taste of earning his own living.

BOX 3A
Legal formalities affecting wills

If you die "intestate"—without a will—the laws of your home state will divide your property among your spouse, children, and (sometimes) parents or other relatives. Who gets what proportion varies from state to state. Possibly your state law would apportion your estate exactly the way you'd want if you died now, but the subsequent birth or death of heirs might lead to unsatisfactory results in the future. Aside from that, a will can help cut red tape and court costs, while enabling you to specify who'll administer the estate. You also need a will to make use of some of the tax-saving devices discussed in this and other chapters. For similar reasons, your spouse should also have a will, and both wills should provide for the case of a common disaster.

To get the advantages of a will, it must comply strictly with the formalities of your state law. Otherwise, you risk having the will voided and dying intestate. No matter how simple you think your will may be, it should be drawn by a competent attorney. The will should be signed before three witnesses, even if your state requires only two. (Witnesses need not read the will.) It's best—and usually legally necessary—that the witnesses not be your beneficiaries (or their spouses); if your will leaves a witness anything, most states won't allow him to take it. Choose witnesses who'll likely outlive you and be easy to find when needed.

You can dispense with witnesses if the will is "holographic"—entirely in your handwriting—but such a will is prone to error or misinterpretation and may not be acceptable in your state. However, even a nonholographic will can be probated if none of the witnesses to it can be located, though extra red tape is involved. (Some states allow witnesses to make an affidavit at the time the will is signed, sparing an appearance later.)

Although you're reasonably free to dispose of your estate as you wish, state laws generally specify that a minimum share must go to your spouse. The term "dower" is sometimes applied to the wife's right to a share and "curtesy" to the husband's right. No state except Louisiana requires you to leave anything to each of your children, but your will may have to disinherit them explicitly if that's what you intend. Some states also limit the share you can leave to charity at the expense of your kin. And every state outlaws "perpetuities" by limiting the length of time property can remain in trust before being distributed. Failure to observe these rules in drawing your will could cause it to be overturned or modified in court.

The law in some states distinguishes between "separate property" owned by a husband or wife prior to their marriage and "community property" acquired during the marriage from the earnings of either spouse or common funds. Only half the community property can be disposed of in the will of either spouse. It's not always easy to determine which assets fall into each class, but their status can generally be fixed by agreement between husband and wife in case of doubt.

In some circumstances, it may be suitable for a husband and wife to have identical (or reciprocal) wills. If so, they should be separate documents, signed by each spouse individually. A joint or mutual will in the form of a single document signed by both might cost less to draw up, but is almost sure to cause legal or tax problems later on. As pointed out in this chapter, a premarital agreement or Q-TIP trust is frequently a better solution.

By leaving all property for under-age beneficiaries in trust, you can avoid the red tape and restrictions involved in guardianships. And you can specify at what age and in what form your children will inherit. Remember that you're not locked into any decision you make. As your children grow and you get a better idea of how they're shaping up, you can change your will accordingly.

If you have a child you suspect may never be ready to manage an inheritance—a gambler, an alcoholic, or just a plain ne'er-do-well—you can set up a trust to control the principal of his legacy for his lifetime. It needn't be rigid. You can give the trustee, perhaps consulting with a designated member of the family, discretion to decide when and if the child is ready to take over control of the full amount. After all, a son or daughter who has spent the last four years backpacking around the globe could settle down to a responsible job and no longer need a trustee as a caretaker.

Keep these things in mind when you're designing trusts for children: Your trustee should have the flexibility to use not only income but also principal to meet the child's needs. Income alone may not cover soaring college costs or unusual medical bills.

You may also want to include guidelines to help the trustee. If you yourself regretted not having money for a year abroad after college, or for a down payment on a house, or to set up your own practice, you might spell out in your will that you want the principal to be used for such purposes.

Should you treat your children alike?

In nearly every case, the answer is an emphatic Yes. That avoids needless family discord. For instance, a New England internist left his practice, equipment, and other professional property to one of his sons, who was his partner. Then he divided the rest of his estate equally among all four of his children. That may have seemed a practical thing for a father to do, but that's not the way the doctor's other three children saw it. They were sure that their brother had used undue influence on their father. Though they didn't try to contest the will, they did something more lasting: They severed all relations with the innocent beneficiary.

To treat your children equally takes careful thought. If there are special things you want one child to have, you can use cash bequests to equalize the amounts the others will receive. No one's nose would have been out of joint if the internist's will had provided that, before the rest of the estate was divided, each of his other three children should receive amounts equal to the value of the medical assets he left his doctor son.

You may also want to adjust your bequests to offset large disparities in lifetime outlays you've made for some of your children—e.g., for education costs or wedding expenses. Sometimes, however, unequal treatment can't be straightened out in your will. A case in point: Shortly before he died, a retired doctor changed his savings account to a joint account with one of his three daughters. He did it simply for convenience in case he became disabled, but the bank balance went to her when he died. As a result, she got $25,000 more than his other two daughters, even though his will stated that his estate was to be divided equally among all three.

The moral: Make sure that whatever passes outside your will—jointly held property, trust bank accounts, insurance and retirement benefits, for example—will go to your children equally. Or provide for legacies in your will to equalize these amounts, and apportion any estate taxes fairly.

When there's a handicapped child in the family, parents have to decide whether to carve out a larger share for that child or leave their whole estate in trust for his support, with the other children getting only the excess income from the trust. That's a tough decision.

Besides such known differences in family needs, others may come to light later on. A daughter who's happily married and well provided for today may be divorced and in straitened circumstances five years from now. A son who's healthy, active, and on his way to success could be crippled in a future automobile accident.

If you could be sure you'd always be around to help your children, you wouldn't need to put someone else in your shoes. But you won't always be, and a special kind of trust may be required to accommodate your family's requirements should they be highly unpredictable or out of the ordinary.

You set up such a trust by giving your trustee the power to pay out varying amounts of income and principal according to the individual needs of your children or other beneficiaries. Because the trustee has the power to "sprinkle" the money, such a trust is called a sprinkling trust.

According to the directions you give him, the trustee will stand in financially for a parent—helping this child when he gets in trouble, encouraging that child to go into a business venture or to study, withholding from a third who doesn't need help or will do better without it. And by allowing the trustee to provide extra income for the beneficiaries who need it and, presumably, are in lower tax brackets, the sprinkling arrangement can save on income taxes.

If your decision comes down in favor of need over equal treatment, tell your children what you've done and why. Don't let them learn about it when the will is probated. That surprise can prompt sibling rivalry in the most generous of persons—who might have agreed willingly to accept smaller shares than their brothers and sisters if the matter had been discussed with them.

Do your grandchildren need a share?

Suppose one of your children dies before you do. What will happen to his share of your estate? Will it go to *his* own children or to *your* other offspring? In most instances, a doctor would want it to go to his grandchildren, and he may accordingly have to make trust arrangements in his will for them (see Chapter 2).

At this point, one of two legal concepts comes into play: *per stirpes* or *per capita*. Here's an illustration of the difference:

Suppose a physician has two married children who will inherit the estate. The first has one child; the other, three. Let's further suppose that the doctor outlives both children, so that the estate passes to the four grandchildren. If he specifies that they are to inherit per capita, the executors or trustees will count heads and divide the property equally among the four grandchildren. But if the will specifies per stirpes, the distribution will be "by the roots"; i.e., half the estate will go to the grandchild who was an only child and the other half will be divided in three equal shares among the other grandchildren. Neither method is necessarily better than the other, but you must choose one of them.

You may want to leave something to your grandchildren, whether your children survive or not. A legacy of $5,000 or $10,000 isn't just a token of love and affection for the grandchild; it's also a boon to the parents. That money, subject to minimal income taxes over the years, will grow until it's used for the grandchild later on. There's another benefit, too: As pointed out in Chapter 2, most states' tax laws grant exemptions for small bequests to family members. Over the exempt amount, many states base inheritance taxes on what each recipient gets; thus, the more recipients, the less the state taxes.

Can your parents manage alone?

If you're now contributing to the support of a parent, you'll certainly need to set up some kind of arrangement to continue that support. You can do so by leaving an outright bequest, setting up a trust, or directing your executor—in your will—to purchase an annuity for your parent.

Even if your parents are self-sufficient when you make your will, give some thought to their future circumstances. Maybe inflation will gnaw away at that ample pension—or a long illness will use up their assets.

If a doctor has a trust in his will for his children, he can protect his parents by including them as beneficiaries. That can be done by giving the trustee discretionary power to use money from the trust for the parents' support, or by giving specific instructions. The trustee could, for example, be directed to make up the difference if their private income fell below a stated minimum. You could even gear that minimum to the cost-of-living index to better protect a person with a fixed income in inflationary times. The trustee could also be given discretion to meet emergencies or medical needs by using principal or income from the trust.

Have you left anyone out?

You'll need to take equal care in planning for others who may be dependent on you for support—an elderly aunt or an orphaned nephew, say. And you may want to make specific bequests to other relatives, particularly if you own property that has come down through the family. Besides family, think about friends, employees, and charities. Specific bequests and their likely effects are explored in the next section.

Have you named contingent beneficiaries?

You should decide who your beneficiaries will be if your spouse and children don't survive you. If you don't name beneficiaries in their stead, the law in your state will decide. Contingent beneficiaries are also necessary when an estate plan includes a trust. Consider a 45-year-old surgeon who sets up his estate to benefit his wife and their two-year-old daughter without providing for contingent beneficiaries. If the doctor and his wife die, the trust for their daughter is to run until she's 40 or to pass to her children if she dies sooner. But if the daughter should die childless before she reaches the age of 40, the doctor's estate will pass to those relatives who happen to be alive at the time, whether he cared about them or not. Some of them may not even have been born when he died.

Your will should also designate alternate executors, guardians, and trustees as appropriate.

SPECIFIC BEQUESTS: HANDLE WITH CARE

Your current will may provide specific amounts for a favorite niece, a faithful employee, a worthy charity, and other persons or organizations. Examine those bequests in the light of inflation to see whether they'll be large enough to reflect the degree of love, gratitude, or obligation you feel. Even more important, weigh the impact of such bequests on your *residuary legatees*—those who will get the remainder of your estate. Chances are, they're your spouse and children, the ones whose future welfare is uppermost in your mind.

The bequests you specify must be paid out before the balance of your estate is distributed, unless you provide otherwise. With persistent inflation, your residuary estate could prove insufficient to support your family in the style you'd like. So you may want to play it safe by reducing or eliminating the amounts you leave to others. Alternatively, you could make those bequests contingent on a minimum amount being left for your immediate family. That gives the family priority while providing for all beneficiaries if your estate turns out to be large enough.

Even then, specific legacies could be a problem if your estate is short of cash. State laws usually require the estate to pay interest if cash bequests aren't distributed within a set period. The interest comes out of the residuary estate—your family's part. If you don't want your executor to have to choose between paying interest and liquidating assets to avoid it, simply say in your will that the legacies aren't entitled to interest. Your will should also make clear who's to pay the estate taxes on the legacies. (If it doesn't, the oversight could cost your spouse dearly; see Chapter 2.) And be sure to spell out what's to be done with a specific bequest if the beneficiary dies before you.

Aside from those general considerations, some bequests involve special problems you can avoid:

Bequests to office staff and other employees

Unless an assistant has been with you a long time, you'd normally want her to receive a legacy only if she were still working for you at the time of your death. If your will simply gave your nurse, Sarah Smith, $500, she'd collect the inheritance even though she had quit without notice two years before you died. You could hedge by making the gift to your nurse without naming her, but that legacy might go to someone you had hired just a few days before your death. So to reward a faithful assistant, make the gift conditional by such wording as this: "To my nurse, Sarah Smith, provided she is in my employ at the time of my death."

Bequests to charities

Gifts to charity are exempt from estate tax, but not all nonprofit organizations qualify as charities. For example, a doctor left an interest in a trust under his will to his state medical society. The court denied his estate a charitable deduction for the gift because the society's activities include promoting the welfare of its members, influencing legislation, and running a referral service. If an organization doesn't qualify as a charity, someone will have to pay the taxes on the legacy it receives. It's up to you to decide who.

Be certain, by the way, that you list the charity's name correctly in your will. A gift to the "National Institute for Tired Doctors" could result in an expensive court fight between the National Institute for Tired Physicians and the American Association of Tired Doctors.

If you'd like a charitable bequest to be used for a specific purpose, make sure the charity is able and willing to use it in that way. Suppose your legacy to your medical school specifies that the money is to be spent on cancer research. By the time you die, the school may have a pressing need to use the funds for other projects. A good way to avoid such awkward situations is to leave the money unconditionally but with a request that your preferences for its use be taken into consideration. Or you can direct your executor to switch from the charity your will names to another one doing the work you want to support, if your original choice can't use the money as you'd intended.

Bequests of securities

It usually isn't wise to leave specific securities to your beneficiaries. You might later sell some of your holdings, and thus cut off an heir unintentionally. Future stock splits can cause trouble, too. Suppose you leave a cousin 100 shares of Amalgamated Industries, but it splits 3-for-1 before you die. Do you want your cousin to get 100 shares or 300? If your will doesn't make this sort of thing crystal clear, a probate judge might have to decide.

Bequests of medical libraries

Since medical books have little resale value, it may be better to leave your library to another physician or to a school, hospital, or other institution. Instead of saddling a colleague with your entire collection, including out-of-date volumes and duplications of his own books, consider allowing him to select the ones he wants and then letting your executor dispose of the rest.

If you plan to leave your library to a school or medical organization, find out first whether they want the gift. Your medical society may welcome a collection of books in a subspecialty but reject the standard texts and treatises.

Sentimental bequests

Personal property such as sports equipment, records, or jewelry may have great value for you, but it can be a headache for your executor, especially if your will strews your belongings among your friends and relatives. Each beneficiary must be formally notified of his gift and must sign a release when he receives it. All of the items have to be inventoried, and certain pieces that have no readily ascertainable market value may have to be appraised after your death to satisfy the tax authorities. It's possible that, some time before your death, the samurai sword you left your best friend may have disappeared or the easel and paints bequeathed to your partner may have been hauled off by the trash collector. If the specific property no longer exists, your legacy is an empty one.

It's usually better to bequeath all small items to one person—your wife or an adult child, for instance—and to leave a letter with your will listing the friends and relatives to whom you want the items distributed. That not only reduces red tape but also lets you make changes without revising your will. And if you happen to forget that you no longer own the pocket watch you're leaving to Uncle Oliver, your wife or whoever is going to distribute the items can find another appropriate memento to give him.

Bequests of art objects and other valuables

When you're leaving specific property of more than sentimental or nominal value, you should think about what you want done if it's destroyed, lost, or sold between the time you sign your will and your death. If you're leaving your stamp collection to your son only because he will appreciate and enjoy it more than anyone else you know, you needn't arrange for him to get the collection's equivalent in cash in the event that you don't own the stamps at your

What can the custodial parent do about providing for a guardian in the will if the other parent isn't fit to raise the child? A natural parent has prior right to be guardian over everyone else, unless he or she has released the child for adoption. Even if a court of law has judged a parent not competent to be awarded custody, the decision isn't irreversible.

Take the case of a doctor awarded custody of his children whose former wife has been fighting a battle against alcoholism with varying degrees of success. He can name a guardian in his will, but if the children's mother opposes the appointment and seeks custody, she'll probably get it if she's in one of her sober periods. All the doctor can do is name his choice for guardian and hope either that the ex-wife doesn't oppose it, or that the court finds her unfit and recognizes the doctor's choice.

---

death. But if it's part of a plan of equal gifts for all your children, you'd probably want to make it up to your son if the collection were lost or destroyed before your death. Unless you specified in your will that he was to receive the insurance proceeds or the value of the stamp collection in cash, your son would get nothing.

CHILDREN'S GUARDIANS

One of the saddest results of poor estate planning—psychologically as well as monetarily—is failing to designate a guardian for minor children. This becomes important when both parents die simultaneously, when one dies leaving an incapacitated spouse, when the surviving spouse dies while the children are still minors, and in states where the law gives the surviving spouse guardianship of the children's persons but not of their property. (If you are divorced, see Box 3B.)

To minimize this problem, your will can specify both a guardian for the children's personal care if your spouse doesn't outlive you, and another guardian for the children's property, unless you're lucky enough to know someone who's skilled in both child-raising and money management. The property guardian you name is entitled to a fee, may require a bond, and is hemmed in by legal restrictions. But at least *you,* not a court, will have been the one to pick the guardian.

In many cases, the best solution is to name a personal guardian and set up a trust for the children's estate. The trustee gets a fee, of course, but he has far more discretion than a guardian to dispose of property without getting court sanction. And he doesn't have to be bonded, so the total expense should be lower. A guardianship ends when a child becomes 18; a trust can last until whatever age you choose.

Parents are often less confident about the selection of personal guardians than about property guardians or trustees. Here are some steps you can take to reduce the chances of making a mistake or an impractical arrangement:

Ask the children

The first question is obvious: "With whom will the child be happiest?" The answer is usually a judgment call, but too often parents overlook a very important source of help. A New York obstetrician and his wife had narrowed their choice down to his two sisters, but couldn't decide between them. Despite a reluctance about discussing their deaths with their 10- and 13-year-old sons, they asked the boys' opinions. Much to the parents' surprise, there was no fear or tears. Their sons' first concern was whether, without their parents around, there would be enough money to support them. After being assured that there would be, the boys objectively compared their aunts' good and bad points, including their husbands, children, pets, personalities, and lifestyles. Then they rendered their mutual decision. So if your children are mature enough, you should ask them to help pick their guardian.

Don't surprise the guardian

Another person who should always be consulted is the prospective guardian. Someone who's not prepared to take on the job when the time comes may do so grudgingly or even refuse the responsibility.

In talking to a prospective personal guardian, you may encounter some anxiety at first. People may worry that they'll also have to manage your assets—or, worse, dip into their own pockets to support your children. You can dispel this fear by going over the financial aspects of your will, explaining how the trustee will manage the estate and provide money for the youngsters' expenses.

In selecting a married person to act as guardian, parents tend also to name the spouse as co-guardian. There's nothing wrong with having a couple serve as co-guardians, provided it is a deliberate decision and not one made because you think it's the proper thing to do.

Have a backup

Whether you select a single guardian or co-guardians, you should always name at least one alternate. Guardians-elect can die, become ill, get divorced, or for some other reason not be able to assume the role when the time comes. A substitute should also be named out of consideration for the primary guardian. If he isn't in a good position to take on the guardianship when called upon, he may feel compelled to do it anyway if no one else is named. Here's what one couple did: A New York cardiologist and her husband have two children, ages three and five. Today, they would like her mother and father, who are in their mid-50s, to be the guardians. However, the parents realize that in 10 more years, these grandparents will be approaching retirement and might not want the responsibility of overseeing two vigorous teenagers. So the will names two younger alternates. The family has talked over the matter, and the seniors understand that, with substitute guardians available, they can decline the job.

Take care of extra costs for the guardian

In addition to selecting the right people as guardians, you'll want to make sure your offspring won't be a burden to their new family. The trustee will provide money for the child's day-to-day support, so the guardians won't be saddled with such direct costs as medical expenses, tuition, food, and clothing. But the addition of children to a household can impose an economic burden on the substitute parents that could adversely affect the family's standard of living.

For example, a Chicago physician has two children, and his brother, who has three of his own, has agreed to serve as personal guardian. But the brother's house is too small for five kids. In order not to force the family to live in cramped quarters, the doctor's will has a provision authorizing the trustee to contribute to the cost of adding an extension to the house or buying a larger one.

Another physician with a two-year-old son named his sister as guardian. She's vice president of a bank, her children are in their teens, and she hires part-time domestic help. Since the addition of a toddler to her family would require a full-time nurse or housekeeper, the doctor's will directs his trustee to pay any additional household costs his sister may incur in the care of his child.

Let responsibilities overlap

The responsibilities of the personal guardian and the property guardian or trustee having charge of the child's financial security shouldn't always be mutually exclusive. Suppose, for example, you name a bank as trustee. Do you want the trust officers, who are probably strangers, to decide for what purpose and in what amounts funds should be spent for your children, over and above their support? If not, you could spell out in the will what you intend the money to be used for. You might direct that funds be made available for unlimited education, setting up a business, or opening a professional office. The will might get even more specific and try to list large permissible expenditures such as summer camp, travel, or a marriage gift.

However, there's a limit to the number of things a physician can spell out in his will. A better solution may be to shift some of the spending responsibility from the trustee to the personal guardian. The lines of authority aren't absolute. The investment and money management duties can remain with the trustee, but the doctor's will—or the trust document—can give the personal guardian the right to determine how, when, and for what purposes the trust money will be spent.

HEADING OFF A WILL CONTEST

Even in the most harmonious of families, there's always the possibility that someone may try to upset your plans by contesting your will or by making a claim against your estate. That can happen because your estate plan doesn't allow for the unforeseen, or because you yourself have inadvertently set the stage for litigation. Either way, the results can range from higher costs and delays in distributing the estate to squabbles that split the family and defeat your intentions. But you and your lawyer can take steps to see that such possibilities don't occur.

Excluding a spouse

An obvious setup for potential trouble is the will that cuts out a "natural object of one's bounty"—a wife or child. The law generally makes it difficult to disinherit such people altogether. In the case of a spouse, it's flatly impossible in most states. Those states give a surviving husband or wife the right to some part of the estate. So if a doctor leaves his wife out of his will or leaves her less than his state's law allows her, she can claim her portion. If she wins, her share will be carved out of the property going to the other beneficiaries, often disrupting the doctor's plans for those other heirs. In some states, a wife can be left less by bequest in a will than she could get if she were cut out altogether and claimed her share under the state's law. But in every state, obviously, it's important to make certain that state law won't undermine or destroy your estate plan.

Usually, when a husband and wife are legally separated, the wife can't claim a spouse's statutory share. Then he needn't include her in his will. That would also be true if she had been guilty of misconduct, but you'd better leave the executor sufficient evidence to defeat the claim she might make. If she had walked out, for instance, her farewell note could help prove who had abandoned whom. Or mail-order divorce papers she'd sent could counter any claim she might lay to a marital share.

Excluding a child

A parent can disinherit his children in almost every state, but it has to be done the proper way. For example, a child born after his father executes a will is ordinarily entitled to the same share of the estate he'd have received if the father had died without a will. The chief exceptions to that rule occur when it's clear that the child was omitted intentionally or was provided for in some other way. In a number of states, that same rule applies to children who were alive when the will was signed. So to disinherit a child beyond question, it's necessary to say in the will that you're doing so.

Suppose a father wants to cut off his daughter. Does he have to leave her a token bequest? No, just naming her is sufficient. It may even be the wiser course. Rather than "I leave my daughter, Alice, $1," which she may take as an insult that goads her to contest the will, a more judicious clause would be one like "I have made no provision for my daughter, Alice, because she does not need my help"—if, indeed, she unquestionably doesn't. Otherwise, the clause should simply state "no provision."

Even in a state where the father need not mention a living child to disinherit him, it's a good idea to do so anyway. One crusty old Southern MD who had been estranged from his only child for some 25 years told his lawyer that he had no children; as far as he was concerned, his son was dead. In contesting the will, the son claimed that since the doctor didn't know he had a child, he plainly lacked the mental capacity to make a will. So if there's any possibility that a question of competency might be raised, the listing of all next of kin and their relationships in a will can be important evidence that its maker was able to recognize the natural objects of his bounty.

Children of a previous marriage

When a physician with children remarries, the specter of potential estate litigation arises. And the potential problems multiply if his new wife has children of her own or if children are born of the second marriage.

When two people plan to marry and each wants to leave property to his or her own children or relatives, the best arrangement is a premarital agreement. In it, each gives up his rights to the other's estate. Then the survivor can't claim whatever spouse's share state law might otherwise call for.

What about the doctor who wants to provide for his second wife, but at the same time would like to be sure that the children of his earlier marriage will get his estate at her death? He can set up a standard bypass trust with the income going to his wife and the principal to his children when she dies. Normally that would subject the trust to a tax bite at the doctor's death, but his executor can claim the full marital deduction for it under certain conditions. The wife must get all the income from the trust, payable at least yearly, and her right to it must not end for any reason—including marriage—as long as she lives. At her death, the trust property is treated for tax purposes as part of her estate, just like any property left to her outright, even though she can't dispose of it in her own will.* This arrangement is known as a Q-TIP trust—an acronym for "Qualified Terminable-Interest Property."

---

*Her will can specify that any estate tax due on the property be paid out of the trust fund.

Potential troublemakers

Though an estate fight is usually hard to foresee, sometimes circumstances or personalities give an advance clue. Then there are steps you can take to forestall trouble. Take the case of a physician with three daughters who wants to leave the bequest for one of them in trust. Since she suffers from a severe case of "middle childness," she's likely to resent being treated differently from her sisters. How does the doctor prevent her from attacking his will? If state law permits, he could use what is known as an *in terrorem* clause. In effect, it provides that if a beneficiary disputes or contests the will and loses, he forfeits his bequest. The risk of losing everything if the will is sustained can prove an effective deterrent.

For the *in terrorem* clause to be effective, the potential troublemaker must obviously be a beneficiary—somebody who has something to lose. Occasionally, it may be wise to include next of kin in the will just for the purpose of hanging the forfeiture clause on them. One bachelor doctor, for example, has a major surprise in store for his sister and brother, his next of kin. He's leaving the bulk of his estate to a "friend." His family will probably rise up in moral indignation and be tempted to contest the will, claiming undue influence. To cool their ire and make them think twice before filing objections, the doctor is leaving his brother and sister each $10,000, with a forfeiture clause. He believes that's just enough to keep them from taking the risk of losing the bequest.

Proof of competence

When an ill or elderly person executes his will, the state of his mental or physical health can lay the groundwork for claims of incompetence, undue influence, or fraud. A handwritten letter to his attorney, containing instructions about the will, could later help sustain its provisions. And he might ask his physician to be present at the execution of the will itself, because the latter could testify to his mental condition at that crucial time.

In such a situation, the testator's attorney may spend a good deal of time chatting with him and asking questions in front of the witnesses to the signing of the will. Even if they know him well, his condition at the moment of execution is the decisive factor. The lawyer might also ask any beneficiaries to leave the room at the start of the conference, fearing that their presence could lead to a later claim of undue influence.

Oral promises

The doctor who promises to leave someone a bequest in return for services may be bestowing a lawsuit on his executor. It may be a widowed physician who says to his daughter, "If you take care of me, I'll leave you the house when I die,'' or one who tells his niece, "Look after my investments and financial affairs and you'll get half my estate." Though it's only an oral promise, if the expectant beneficiary can prove it was made, she can win her case.

The way to avoid that problem is to make neither promises nor statements that could be interpreted as promises. If you want such an arrangement or have already made a promise, the agreement should be put in writing and signed by both you and the recipient of your gift.

Insulting language

Don't include statements in your will such as: "I make no provision for my brother because he is a blankety-blank." The satisfaction of venting your spleen now isn't worth the potential cost to your heirs. For one thing, you risk exposing the estate to a suit for defamation. But even statements that are something less than libelous can cause trouble. Many will fights are brought more in anger than greed, and it's foolish to set out to stir up bad feelings. So before you decide to take a slap at someone in your will, consider the possible consequences and head off the fight over your estate when it can best be stopped—before it starts.

SAVING TROUBLE WITH CODICILS

A codicil is the legal term for a statement—often only a sentence or two—that modifies or adds to an existing will. Codicils can frequently spare you the time and money needed to overhaul your entire will. But keep in mind that, to be legally effective, the codicil must be executed with all of the formalities of the will itself. In most states, it must be dated and signed by you in the presence of witnesses who then sign or "attest to" your signature. The lawyer's fee will usually be modest, assuming he's the one who drafted the original will.

Be warned, though, that sometimes a codicil is the wrong approach. Your lawyer may insist on rewriting the entire will if he thinks a codicil could open a Pandora's box or if you've already tacked on several of them. So the chief rule when adding an afterthought is this: Keep it short and sweet. Here are some of the most common situations in which a codicil is usually sufficient—along with related situations where a completely new will would make more sense:

Naming a new executor, trustee, or guardian

Say the one you named has died, or you simply want somebody else to do the job—for example, one of your children who's now grown up. This can readily be done by codicil.

Obviously, you're not going to hurt the feelings of a bank if you substitute your son as executor. But think twice about using a codicil if your original will named your Uncle Arthur, who's still living. He could be embarrassed or angered when your will is probated and the fact that you replaced him is made public. He might also be required to waive his original role as executor. So consider writing a new will that never mentions him.

Revalidating your will

Suppose you move several hundred miles away. A lawyer in your new locality tells you your will is still valid but getting hold of the witnesses could be a problem. In some states, you can simply sign a codicil that "republishes" or revalidates your original will. The codicil witnesses could then testify at the probate of your will. A similar codicil could serve your purpose if the original witnesses, rather than you, have moved away.

Dropping a beneficiary

When you drew up your will, you may have left $20,000 to your Aunt Margaret. She's since died, and you're not so close to her children that you'd want them to get the money. If your will doesn't already provide for an automatic revocation when a beneficiary dies, you can revoke the gift by codicil and direct that it shall become part of your residuary estate.

But what if Margaret hasn't died—and the real reason you're cutting her out is a family feud? Then rewriting the entire will to eliminate any mention of her is the best course. Otherwise, she'll learn at probate of the original legacy, and she'll have a legal right to contest the codicil's validity.

If there have been some additions to the family

Suppose you had no grandchildren when you made your will, and now there are three. Though your primary concern is to take care of your wife and children, you'd like to be remembered through a token gift to each grandchild. It's easy to add a codicil bequeathing "$5,000 to each of my grandchildren who shall be living at the date of my death."

Why not list the grandchildren by name? Because your children may present you with additional heirs. If so, you'd unintentionally disinherit them. The word "each" solves your problem. And if you don't like the idea of making gifts to anybody but your children's own kids, you can word the codicil to exclude their stepchildren or adopted children. It should probably exclude illegitimate children also, to lessen the chance of a will contest.

When you want to cancel an intrafamily debt

Let's say you've just lent your son and his wife $30,000 for the down payment on their first house. If you die before the loan is repaid, you wouldn't want them to be forced to pay your estate. A codicil can assure that any outstanding balance on the loan will be canceled.

These aren't the only situations in which adding a codicil is preferable to scrapping your entire will. New assets could call for adjustments. The same goes for property you've disposed of. Suppose you designated your son to inherit a plot of land that you since have sold. What, if anything, do you want to give him instead? You may be able to clear up questions like that with a codicil. *But make sure your lawyer approves the wording.*

4

Spare your heirs administrative problems and expense

It's not only taxes that shrink an estate. You can figure that the administrative expenses will run from 5 to 8 percent of your estate's value if you leave between $500,000 and $1 million. Those outlays include your executor's and attorney's fees, court costs, accounting fees, debts, and any miscellaneous administrative expenses.

If you haven't buttoned up your estate neatly, administrative fees can take a bigger percentage. So give thought to what you can do now to make the administration of your estate as easy and economical as possible.

YOUR PROBATE ESTATE

The more readily an estate can be probated, the lower its legal and accounting costs will be. An outdated will—or no will at all—is bound to kite administrative costs by complicating the estate settlement. Even if your present will spells out your latest ideas plainly, a review session every couple of years will focus your attention on any problems that may have cropped up with the passage of time. Some that could drag out the settlement are a dead beneficiary, a reluctant executor, a change in federal or state laws. (A checklist to help you review your will appears in Appendix 1.)

The probate estate is the property that passes directly via your will, and the amount of it has a bearing on your estate settlement costs. Executor's commissions, for example, are usually based on the size of the probate estate, not the gross estate. Probate estate value may also influence the fees attorneys charge, though that's not so likely. Local laws and customs vary, but properties that pass outside the will—such as life insurance, living trusts, jointly owned assets, and gifts—are apt to reach your heirs with less shrinkage.

Suppose you pulled $30,000 out of your potential probate estate and gave it to your heirs right now. It could save them $1,000 or so in executor's commissions, not to mention legal and administrative fees. Sometimes, of course, legal fees do have to be paid on property transfers outside the will. But usually such transfers are money-savers.

One caveat that applies particularly to larger estates: Reducing the amount of the probate estate could result in higher total taxes under some circumstances. So inform your estate-planning adviser fully about your non-probate assets and consult him before making any major changes in their amount or disposition.

JOINT OWNERSHIP

Moving particular assets to joint ownership now may mean saving costs later—or it could bring more fees and taxes. Remember, if you intend to leave property to your spouse, there is no estate-tax advantage to putting it under joint title. Whether you own it separately or jointly, your spouse will inherit it tax-free, thanks to the unlimited marital deduction. In fact, too much joint property might increase the total estate tax in some cases.

Here's a simplified example: A couple has $600,000 in joint assets, and the husband separately owns $300,000. He dies first, leaving his $300,000 to the children; she gets full ownership of the $600,000 joint property at his death and leaves it to the children at hers. There's a tax credit on each estate. Result: There's no tax on the entire $900,000. Suppose instead that he puts his $300,000 in joint ownership. Then at his death, the whole $900,000 must go to her. The tax credit on her estate later shields only $600,000. Result: $300,000 is taxable when she dies.

However, if you don't carry joint ownership to extremes, or your total estate is small, it can still pay off by reducing the cost of settling your estate. Suppose you have $60,000 in a money-market account when you die. If it goes to your spouse under your will, legal and administrative fees will take a chunk of it—possibly $1,500 or so. But if you duck probate by making it a joint account with right of survivorship, your spouse gets the $60,000 intact.

However, you must be careful which assets you transfer to joint ownership. Say you bought stock for $20,000 that's worth $60,000 at your death. Putting the stock in joint title might save $1,500 in probate fees but could needlessly cost your spouse more than twice that in income tax on the capital gain when she sells it. Here's why: If you're the sole owner of the stock, its cost basis when your spouse inherits it will be $60,000—the value at the date of your death. So there's no capital gain if it's sold for that price. But if the stock is in both names, the law says that you and your spouse each own half, regardless of who paid for it.* The cost basis for the half she inherits is $30,000, its value at your death. The cost of the other half, though, is $10,000—half the $20,000 purchase price. Selling her half for $30,000 nets her a capital gain of $20,000, taxable at a top rate of 20 percent.‡

Clearly, if your only reason for joint ownership is to save estate expenses, it's best to limit it to assets with little or no capital-gain potential, such as bank accounts and certificates of deposit. Assuming the husband is likely to die first, he should remain sole owner of most appreciated properties. You'll probably want to make an exception of your house. The law exempts up to $125,000 of capital gain from tax if a homeowner is over 55, so joint ownership isn't apt to hurt the surviving spouse.

LIVING TRUSTS

It's also possible to remove assets from your probate estate by putting them into a trust while you're alive instead of disposing of them in your will. The trust doesn't have to be irrevocable to accomplish this. You can be your own trustee and maintain full control of the trust assets, adding to them or removing or selling them as you please, just as if there were no trust. You'll be taxed on any income or capital gains while you live, and the trust holdings will be part of your taxable estate at death. But they won't go through probate court proceedings. Rather, the trustee you've appointed to succeed you will distribute them to your heirs in accordance with your instructions. You can change your mind anytime as to who gets what, when, and how. If you like, at your death the trust can be transformed into a bypass trust (see Chapter 2).

Since no court proceeding is required, there's no attorney's fee for probate. It will typically cost about $1,000 to set up such a trust. If you act as trustee, there won't be any significant additional costs until you die. Then there will be trustee's fees to pay, as stipulated in the trust document, unless the successor you've appointed is willing to serve gratis.

Of course, if the bulk of your estate consists of nonprobate assets, such as jointly owned property or insurance and retirement-plan proceeds payable to named beneficiaries, a revocable living trust may have little potential for cost savings. But it might still help your heirs by smoothing the transfer of assets and lowering the chances of probate hassles. Even with a revocable trust, you should have a will to make sure none of your assets go astray.

In some states, you may have to name a co-trustee if you serve as your own trustee. Even if that's not required, you may prefer to make your spouse

---

*The rule is different for joint owners other than husband and wife; see Chapter 11.

---

‡In a community-property state, if the stock is held as community property rather than jointly owned, the cost basis of the survivor's half would be its value at the date of the other spouse's death—$30,000 in this example—eliminating the taxable capital gain on both halves.

Estate planning strategies for physicians

or another heir co-trustee and familiarize him or her with the management of the trust assets.

EXECUTOR'S FEES AND RESPONSIBILITIES

In many states, the maximum fee an executor—or an "administrator" appointed by the court if you die intestate—may charge an estate is set by law. The amount is determined on a sliding scale, so that small estates are charged a higher percentage of their assets than large ones. In some states, though, the law merely says an executor's charges should be "reasonable," and leaves it up to the courts to determine what's reasonable. (For an idea of what executor's fees are in your state, see Box 4A.)

Don't assume that your estate has to pay the maximum fee set by law. If you have a sizable, well-planned estate, you may be able to negotiate a fee below the top figure.

Your estate can save a considerable sum if the person you name as executor agrees to waive the fee, as might be the case with a spouse or trusted friend or relative. But is the saving worth it?

The answer often is No. The executor must manage the business affairs of your estate during the months—or years—from the time you die until your heirs receive the property. He pays your debts and collects your accounts receivable. He sells your practice and equipment if he can, or oversees the sale or transfer of shares in your professional corporation. He collects the income from your investments and perhaps the proceeds of your insurance policies. He sells some of your property, if necessary, to pay taxes. He files the tax returns, writes the checks, and keeps the books, hiring legal and accounting help when needed. And along with all that, he may act as a financial adviser to your family.

Accordingly, most experts believe only a professional executor—lawyer or bank—should handle those responsibilities. A bank trust department or a trust company has the two big advantages of continuity and experience. No matter how many years from now you die, or how long it takes to settle your estate, the bank will probably still be there. Its personnel will have administered thousands of estates like yours, so the settlement should go smoothly.

Perhaps you feel that banks tend to be stodgy and would manage the estate too conservatively. There's something to that feeling—and also to the allegation that banks tend to be insensitive to human emotions when settling estates. An ideal individual executor could probably do more for your heirs than a bank could. But is such a person available to you?

A lawyer has the advantage that he's already involved in your estate plan—or should be. And he may be willing to waive executor's commissions and charge only attorney's fees. Some state laws, in fact, forbid double fees to a lawyer. But a lawyer-executor isn't your best bet unless yours is that rarity

BOX 4A
Executor's fee

The amount an executor may charge for administering an estate varies greatly from state to state. Sliding-scale formulas are used in many states to set the maximum fee for an estate of a given size. In the states marked with an asterisk, the laws simply allow "reasonable" fees, as determined by the courts. While the figures are subject to change, you can get an idea of executor's fees from this state-by-state rundown for administering a $500,000 estate.

	Maximum fee		Maximum fee
Alabama	$25,000	Montana	$10,400
Alaska*	5,000	Nebraska*	10,000
Arizona*	10,000	Nevada	10,120
Arkansas	15,150	New Hampshire*	21,000
California	11,150	New Jersey	25,000
Colorado*	15,000	New Mexico*	25,150
Connecticut*	19,500	New York	19,000
Delaware*	14,000	North Carolina*	25,000
District of Columbia	50,000	North Dakota*	8,000
Florida*	16,500	Ohio	15,000
Georgia	25,000	Oklahoma	12,585
Hawaii	10,310	Oregon	10,630
Idaho*	10,000	Pennsylvania*	15,000
Illinois*	14,000	Rhode Island*	13,000
Indiana*	16,000	South Carolina	25,000
Iowa	10,120	South Dakota	12,585
Kansas*	15,000	Tennessee*	14,000
Kentucky	25,000	Texas	25,000
Louisiana	12,500	Utah*	5,910
Maine*	25,000	Vermont*	15,500
Maryland	21,200	Virginia*	25,000
Massachusetts	15,000	Washington*	12,500
Michigan*	10,050	West Virginia*	25,000
Minnesota*	12,500	Wisconsin	10,000
Mississippi	35,000	Wyoming	10,350
Missouri*	14,050		

*"Reasonable" executor's fees are allowed by courts; the fees shown are believed to be customary or representative.

who combines business acumen, ample time for the work, and a personal interest in your family's welfare. This combination can occasionally be found closer to home in a member of the family. Such a person may have a strong motivation to do right for your heirs. He may also be inclined to waive the executor's commissions. But if he lacks the lawyer's know-how and the bank's experience, his value in settling your estate may be limited.

A compromise that sometimes works well is to appoint a family member as an unpaid co-executor along with a professional executor. You then have continuity, experience, and the personal touch—a package that's probably not to be had in any individual executor. Unlike a bank, an individual executor must be bonded, unless this is waived in your will.

All of the above notwithstanding, you and your spouse may feel more comfortable if she's named sole executor. This leaves her free to seek advice when she needs it, but doesn't force her to accept outside interference, except as the laws require. You may want to recommend an attorney or other advisers, but let her do the choosing when the time comes. While you live, make it a point to involve your wife in your financial affairs, or at least to keep her thoroughly informed about them.

CHOOSING AND INSTRUCTING TRUSTEES

If your estate plan includes a trust, you need to consider carefully not only who the trustee should be, but also how much discretion and guidance to give him. In order to look after the beneficiaries' best interests, the trustee must be able to judge what those interests are—as you would do if you were alive—and have the authority to apply the trust funds appropriately.

Spouse as trustee

The kind of trust you're most likely to provide in your will is one whose income goes to your spouse while she lives, with the principal going to the children thereafter. If you're setting up the trust solely for tax reasons and would have preferred leaving the money outright to your spouse, she would seem to be your logical choice as trustee. However, as both a beneficiary and the trustee of your estate, she may face legal restrictions that wouldn't apply to an independent trustee.

For instance, you may want to give the trustee broad power to dip into principal for the benefit of your wife or children. But if your wife is the trustee, the IRS might argue that you've given her the power to say where the trust principal goes. Such a ''general power of appointment'' makes the principal taxable as part of her estate—just what you're trying to avoid with the trust.

Naming your spouse trustee may also spring an income-tax trap. Even if she's likely to have ample income outside the trust, you may still want to allow the trustee to pay her the trust income if her circumstances change for the worse. Assuming she doesn't need that money, there could be a sizable income-tax saving if the trustee accumulates it or uses it for the children. But if *she's* the trustee, all the income will be taxable to her whether she takes it or not, because she has the ability to do so.

Those drawbacks needn't rule out your spouse as trustee, but they call for careful consideration of applicable state and federal laws by your attorney.

Independent trustee

If you opt for an independent trustee, what qualifications should you require? Basically, you must be convinced that the trustee has the expertise to manage the trust's assets satisfactorily or can be relied on to obtain sound financial advice. Equally necessary, your trustee must know or learn enough about your family to act in their best interests, making appropriate use of the powers you've given him. The more discretion you want him to exercise, the larger that latter criterion looms.

If you expect the trustee to replace you as head of the family in financial matters, make sure that he understands the nature of his responsibilities and is willing and able to undertake them. One Chicago doctor named a close friend as trustee for his four children, and gave him power to distribute funds among them as needed, rather than on an equal-shares basis. At first, the trustee tried to carry out his assignment faithfully, granting or denying the children's requests as he felt their father would have done. But constant pressure and accusations of favoritism and unfairness wore him down. Now he treats all the beneficiaries alike, ignoring the doctor's intentions.

While an institutional trustee such as a bank may take a more impersonal attitude toward your beneficiaries, it may be a better choice in some cases, especially when the trust is a large one and its management involves a lot of time and paperwork. Banks also have the advantage of longer life and more permanent location than individuals; extensive experience in handling estates; and the assurance of government supervision of their activities.

Bank trust fees are generally based on the value of the trust's assets, commonly running between 0.5 and 1 percent a year; there may also be a termination fee. Some banks charge according to a sliding scale; others charge a minimum annual fee, or refuse a trust worth less than a specified amount. A bank might also be unwilling to accept a trust involving the operation of a business, or else insist on a higher fee. Such matters should be ironed out before selecting a particular bank as trustee.

If you decide on a bank trustee, you can inject a personal element by choosing an individual as co-trustee. Or you might name the bank as sole trustee, but require it to consult with, or get the approval of, an individual under certain conditions—say, when expenditure of trust principal is in question. That arrangement permits you to appoint someone who knows the beneficiaries well and is concerned with their happiness and well-being.

Discretionary powers

Whether the trust is controlled by an individual, a bank, or both, you must decide how much discretion to give the trustee. He can have unlimited power to pay out income and principal, or you can put a dollar or percentage limitation on the amount paid to one beneficiary or to a class of beneficiaries (e.g., "my married daughters"). Alternatively, you can provide guidelines for the trustee instead of restrictions—for example, that the beneficiaries' earnings and other resources be considered in allocating trust income.

Estate planners caution against being too specific in your instructions to the trustee. The longer a trust is likely to last, the greater the odds of unforeseeable events occurring, so that your instructions will fail to reflect your intentions. One solution is to allow the trustee very broad discretion in the trust document, but give him a letter setting forth guidelines and explaining your purposes. The letter can also provide the trustee with confidential information about the various beneficiaries to help him make decisions.

In addition, consider authorizing the trustee to terminate the trust if it dwindles to where it becomes inefficient or uneconomical to continue it. A bank's minimum annual fees, for example, might well eat up half or more of the income from a trust whose principal is in the $50,000 to $100,000 range.

Beneficiaries' powers

There's another way to build flexibility into a trust or protect beneficiaries against a trustee who might interpret your instructions too rigidly. You can empower a beneficiary to withdraw trust principal, provided you're not so liberal that you jeopardize the tax and other benefits of the trust.

Suppose your will sets up a standard bypass trust, where your spouse gets life income and your children inherit the principal at her death. You can allow her the right to take annually up to 5 percent of the trust principal or $5,000, whichever is more. Provided the power isn't cumulative—e.g., she can't skip one year and take 10 percent the next—the trust fund won't be taxed in her estate.

You could even grant your spouse the power to dictate in her will how the trust principal is to be divided among your children. That's called a "special power of appointment" and doesn't alter the tax status of the trust. The rationale behind it is that, after surviving for some years, your spouse will have a better idea of whom the money will do the most good than you could have foretold.

It may also be worthwhile to allow the beneficiary to change trustees if specified conditions arise—for instance, if the beneficiary moves to another state. A beneficiary can convince a court to remove a trustee because of wrongdoing or gross negligence, but not merely because of disagreements or general dissatisfaction.

Consider this example: An anesthesiologist named his 52-year-old brother trustee in his will. The brother was still serving as trustee in his 70s. By then he was out of touch with family affairs, though not incompetent in the eyes of a judge.

To deal with that possibility, especially if you must pick an older person as trustee, you could give your beneficiary the power to appoint additional trustees who can outvote him and take over administration of the trust. You could go further and give the beneficiary the right to remove the trustee without cause. However, if he has broad powers to distribute principal, the IRS could claim that the beneficiary in effect controls the trust. That would make it taxable in the beneficiary's estate, something the trust might have been set up to avoid.

PROVIDING ESTATE LIQUIDITY

Too often, executors are forced to sell stocks, real estate, or other property to pay taxes and claims because there's insufficient ready cash in the estate. Even the most experienced executor is powerless to prevent losses on forced sales. So guard against that kind of estate erosion by giving your executor and your family enough cash and life insurance to work with. (Box 4B can help you determine the amount.) Then your heirs can sell the assets when they want to—not when a tax or bill collector is demanding money.

Keep in mind that your widow will need ready cash, too. She'll fare best if you provide her with $10,000 to $15,000 outside your probate estate, so it won't be entangled in red tape. The simplest way is to earmark a life insurance policy for that purpose—not necessarily a new policy; a current one will probably do as well. Just be sure that your spouse is listed as the beneficiary, and that she will have her choice of settlement options.

Even before the insurance money comes, your widow will probably need to write checks. If you have a joint bank account with her now, ask your banker how long it will be frozen when one owner dies. State laws vary; so do joint accounts. Unless it's certain that your widow will have fast access to yours, better transfer at least $3,000 to a bank account that's in her name alone and make sure it isn't depleted while you're alive.

However you take care of the cash problem, leave a memorandum explaining what you've provided. Attach it to a copy of your will if you want, but don't make it part of your will. That could slow down the fast action you're aiming for.

ORGANIZING YOUR PERSONAL RECORDS

Even if you think you know exactly where all your non-professional records are, you may be the only one who knows. It could prove troublesome and costly if you're not around to help find a document when it's needed quickly.

With the aid of the form shown in Box 4C, you can shape up all your records quickly. Doing this can pay off richly in convenience—perhaps later on for your family, assuredly now for you.

The form suggests where to keep what—balancing security with accessibility—and how long to keep each item. Once you've done your organizing,

BOX 4B
Will your estate have enough cash?

This worksheet will help you answer that question. If it's a close call, you may want to take some of the actions suggested in this chapter and Chapter 7 to improve liquidity.

Cash needs

A. Debts, final expenses, and administrative costs[1] $ _____

B. Estate tax (see Box 2B) _____

C. Cash bequests _____

D. Investment carrying costs[2] _____

E. Family cash needs[3] _____

F. Total estate cash needs (add A through E) $ _____

Liquid assets

G. Bank accounts and other cash-type assets $ _____

H. Lump sums from insurance, etc. _____

I. Marketable securities _____

J. Other readily salable assets _____

K. Total liquid assets (add G through J) $ _____

Cash surplus or deficit (difference between F and K) $ _____

[1]Rough estimate: 7.5 percent of gross estate.
[2]First year's expenses for interest, property taxes, etc., less rental or other income.
[3]First year's family expenses, less income from pensions, annuities, accounts receivable, etc.

you can use the form to record where you've put everything. Simply check off those items you've stored in the recommended places; where necessary, indicate any different locations you've chosen. As noted earlier, it's probably not advisable to dictate in your will the disposition of specific assets. You may no longer own the asset when you die; even if you do, you can't be sure what it will be worth then. The better way is to prepare a lis of your assets separately from your will. Include any information you think will help your executor or trustee to dispose of or manage them. Suggest, for instance, whom to ask for information about selling a sideline business, and what to do about winding it up if it can't be sold.

If you're in solo practice, you'll need to tell your heirs what to do about the assets and how to deal with a number of other problems. (They're discussed in Chapter 9.)

BOX 4C
Where and how long to keep personal records

You'll do yourself and your heirs an important service if you keep a list like this up to date and make sure it will readily be found at your death.

Record	Your location, if different	How long to keep
Keep in safe-deposit box:		
Birth certificates	_____	Permanently
Citizenship papers	_____	Permanently
Marriage and divorce records	_____	Permanently
Passports	_____	Permanently
Military service records	_____	Permanently
Deeds	_____	While current; then to dead storage
Mortgages	_____	While current
Leases	_____	While current plus two years
Title insurance policies	_____	While current
Valuable jewelry	_____	Until disposed of
Stocks and bonds	_____	Until disposed of
Promissory notes	_____	Until paid; then to dead storage
Auto titles, documents	_____	Until sold
Sideline-business agreements	_____	While current; then to dead storage
Keep at attorney's office:		
Originals of wills	_____	While in effect
Powers of attorney	_____	While in effect
Safe-deposit box key (spare)	_____	While rented
Combination to home safe or strongbox	_____	Permanently
Keep in home safe or strongbox:		
Bankbooks	_____	Until account closed; then to dead storage
Duplicates of wills	_____	While in effect
Safe-deposit box key	_____	While rented
Coin and stamp collections	_____	Until disposed of

Estate planning strategies for physicians

Record	Your location, if different	How long to keep
Life insurance policies	_____	While in force
Casualty insurance policies	_____	While in effect; then to dead storage
Keep in desk or file at home:		
Checkbook	_____	While current
Bank statement, deposit slips	_____	While current; then to dead storage
Safe-deposit box inventory	_____	Permanently; update as required
Credit-card numbers	_____	Permanently; update as required
Warranties	_____	While in effect
Personal tax returns (1040)	_____	Six years, then to dead storage
Tax estimates (1040 ES)	_____	Six years, then to dead storage
Canceled checks for deductions	_____	Six years, then to dead storage
Records of tax payments	_____	Six years, then to dead storage
Records of securities held and other investments	_____	Until final tax disposition; then to dead storage
Records of home cost(s) and improvements	_____	Until final tax disposition; then to dead storage

In reviewing your assets, don't forget your personal possessions. What's to be done with your coin collection? Who's to get the family heirlooms, your sports equipment, your library, and so on? The answers can be included in a letter of instructions, telling your family what they need to know in the event of your death or serious disability.

Such a letter should include the names, addresses, and telephone numbers of at least your attorney, accountant, insurance agent, and stockbroker. You might even include a list of recurring bills—like property taxes—with notes on when and how they're to be paid.

Don't make your survivors guess what type of funeral or burial you would want. If you're reluctant to broach the subject with your family, indicate your preferences in writing.

To make your letter of instructions and inventory most useful to your family, you'll have to keep them up to date. Review them whenever there's a major change in your affairs, and make any necessary amendments. It's also a good idea to look them over regularly to be sure that a lot of small changes haven't added up to a big one. A convenient time to do the updating might be after you collect the data for your income tax return.

Finally, be sure to keep the letter and inventory where your family will be certain to find them when they're needed. Your desk at home is a good spot, since you'll want to have this material handy when it needs updating.

5

Plug the gaps
with insurance

Disposing of your assets in an orderly, tax-efficient manner, though important, may not by itself achieve your major estate-planning objective: to provide for the well-being of your family. What if your present resources aren't enough to do the job adequately? Over the years, you may hope to raise your net worth via savings and investments, as discussed in later chapters. But death or disability could rob you of the time you're counting on to increase the size of your estate. Insurance can help you deal with that contingency.

Keep in mind, however, that what you spend on policy premiums reduces the amount of capital you have available for more lucrative investments. The longer you live, the less economical insurance becomes. So you do well to buy only the amount of protection needed to bridge the gap between your resources and your responsibilities. Since that gap will vary as circumstances change, periodic review is called for.

In assessing your current needs, focus on the two main purposes of life insurance: to preserve your family's standard of living and to provide ready cash to pay various estate costs. It's easy to lose sight of those needs when you face the insurance industry's bewildering array of options and jargon. Not only are there traditional life policies, but also universal life, variable life, and assorted hybrid policies that combine features of the others. The basic choice, though, is between term insurance and cash-value ("whole life") insurance. You first need to understand the kinds of available policies, then pick the ones that best meet your situation and your familiy's changing needs.

TERM VS. WHOLE-LIFE COVERAGE

With term insurance, you insure your life just as you do your car—for a given amount of value over a given period. If there's no "loss" during the policy period—that is, if you don't die—the money goes down the drain. There's no savings element. The term is often one or five years, and you can usually renew the policy at the end of the period, but at a higher premium, since your age has put you at higher risk of death. Sometimes the renewal clause is on a guaranteed basis, so that you can continue the insurance irrespective of health, and you also may be able to convert the policy to whole life at a substantially higher premium. The guaranteed and conversion options raise the premium for term insurance.

Term coverage has generally been regarded by financial advisers as a better buy than cash-value life for younger doctors. A term policy can cost a 35-year-old male nonsmoker as little as 60 cents per thousand dollars of coverage. So $500,000 of term protection may run him just $300 a year for the first few years of the policy. The same amount of whole life might cost as much as $8,000 a year.

An agent might point out that a term policy will probably not be renewable beyond age 65 to 70—but you may no longer need it then. The agent will also stress that your whole-life premium remains constant and, in fact, will get lower if there are policy dividends to reduce it. But you pay so much less for term in the early years that the total cost may well be smaller—provided you invest the premium difference.

If you buy whole life, the insurance company will invest part of the premium for you—the cash value—but the rate of return will be less than you can obtain by doing your own investing. This assumes, however, that you invest the premium saving regularly and wisely.

Say the term policy costs you $300 for each of the first five years before the premium rises, compared with $8,000 for whole life. If you can invest the $7,700 annual saving at 10 percent after taxes, you'll have a fund worth about $50,000 at the end of five years. Even though your term premium goes up in the sixth year, and periodically thereafter, you'll still be able to put away some savings. More than the whole-life policy's cash value? Probably. But even if it isn't larger, the fund you set aside from premium savings is always yours. The cash-value fund the insurance carrier sets aside for you is buried in the policy. And when you die, your beneficiary gets the face amount, but the company pockets the cash value.

You can, of course, retrieve the cash value by giving up the policy if you no longer need the coverage. Or you can keep the policy in force and borrow the cash value. The policy is your collateral and you create your own payback schedule. In fact, you don't have to pay the loan back at all, but the outstanding balance will be deducted from the settlement your beneficiaries receive. In older policies, the loan rates may be very attractive, but you might have to pay market rates on loans against newer policies, which are no longer subject to a regulatory ceiling.

NEW KINDS OF POLICIES

To improve the attractiveness of cash-value insurance as an investment, a number of companies have developed variations on traditional whole-life policies. One type, "universal" or "adjustable-premium" life, purports to offer a much higher return than straight life does because the company invests the cash value in high-yield securities, money-market funds, and perhaps even real estate.

After the first premium is paid, the policyholder can pay premiums when and in whatever amount he prefers. He can withdraw part of the cash value without surrendering the policy, or he can borrow against it, just as with whole life. He can increase or reduce the face amount (death benefit) and the policy will remain in force if there is enough cash value to cover monthly administration fees and the cost of protection. (The protection element of a universal-life policy costs perhaps 25 percent more than pure term insurance.)

A universal-life policy generally guarantees only a nominal growth rate—3 or 4 percent—after the first year, but in some years the investment results have been so good that the increase in cash value has substantially exceeded the premium paid in. However, the law sets limits on the tax-free buildup of the cash value in such a policy. If it comes too close to the face value, the law treats the policy as an investment rather than as insurance, making the cash value partially subject to tax.

The younger you are, the lower the permissible ratio of cash value to death benefit. If you have, for example, a $150,000 universal-life policy, the cash value must not exceed $60,000 until you're past 40. At age 55, it can be as high as $100,000; at 65, $125,000.

One way to get around the problem is to raise the death benefit when the cash value nears the limit. But this means more of the premium must be used to pay for the increased insurance. So less goes into the cash fund for investment, and the effective return shrinks.

This difficulty probably won't affect so-called variable-life policies, another interest-sensitive approach to insurance investing. They have a fixed premium and guaranteed death benefit, but cash value is not guaranteed. It waxes and wanes with investment performance.

Variable life isn't as flexible as universal life; you can't vary your premium payment and its distribution between protection and investment. But variable life does allow you to vary the investment vehicle. You select from several options where you want the cash-value part of the premium invested, and you usually can change your vehicle from time to time.

BOX 5A
Compare your life insurance coverage

About 93 percent of all doctors have some form of life insurance. In the 40 to 49 age group, the figure exceeds 97 percent; this group is also the most heavily insured—typically over $300,000. Most physicians under 60 combine term with cash-value coverage. Even in their 60s, a sizable number—three in 10—still retain both types despite the high cost of term in later years.

	% of MDs with that much at age:			
Amount of coverage	39 or younger	40-49	50-59	60 or older
$500,000 or more	25%	27%	10%	4%
300,000 - 499,999	24	26	18	6
200,000 - 299,999	20	24	28	9
150,000 - 199,999	10	7	12	7
100,000 - 149,999	14	9	15	19
Less than $100,000[1]	7	7	17	55
	% of MDs who have it[2] at age:			
Type of coverage	39 or younger	40-49	50-59	60 or older
Term only	24%	19%	16%	17%
Cash value only	18	21	23	47
Both	58	60	61	36

[1]Including those with none.
[2]Excluding those with none.
Source: Medical Economics surveys.

Like other cash-value insurance, variable life doesn't accumulate much in the investment account during the early years. The cost of the protection is a bit lower than for whole life, but a great deal higher than for term.

Though term coverage generally has the edge in cost, a case can be made for cash-value insurance if you have doubts about your ability to save and invest on your own; there may also be tax advantages. Many physicians— three out of five under age 60—have both term and cash-value insurance (see Box 5A). In the end, your choice may be dictated by the total amount of coverage you require.

MATCHING COVERAGE TO CHANGING NEEDS

Some agents say that a married man with two children should have life insurance equal to four times his annual net income. Premiums for this coverage, they add, should total about 6 percent of such income.

But the truest measure of how much life insurance you should carry isn't really your income. It's your dependents' needs that should determine the coverage. How much do you want them to have after you die? How much of that will come from investments and other resources? Only the remainder need come from insurance.

Take 35-year-old Dr. Young, with a wife and two pre-teenage children. His life insurance needs are likely to be far greater than those of 55-year-old Dr. Senior, who has grown children and a large investment nest egg. The only sound way to determine how much coverage to buy is to estimate your family's needs and compare the total with the value of your assets. The size of the shortfall, if any, is the measure of your insurance requirements. (See Box 5B to determine your life insurance needs.)

Family's living expenses

If you weren't around, how much would be needed for the family's food, clothing, home maintenance (excluding mortgage payments), car costs, medical and dental expenses, vacations, entertainment, and taxes? The list in Box 5C can help you get the answer, or you may prefer to estimate it on the basis of your present income. For example, a doctor with pretax income of $75,000 might estimate 30 percent of that for his widow's upkeep plus 10 percent for each dependent child. You can shade those percentages somewhat if your income is substantially higher.

The insurance you provide to support your widow should, of course, be reduced by the amount of other benefits your family would be eligible for, such as Social Security survivors' benefits if you died leaving at least one child under 18 (see Box 5D). A widow with one child could receive around $1,000 a month. The figure may be adjusted for inflation.

Once you decide how much your family would need for living expenses, there's a second judgment to make: Do you want to provide that allowance out of principal plus interest, or out of interest alone, leaving the principal intact for your children to inherit? The latter plan is, of course, considerably more expensive. Using interest only (at 7 percent), $200,000 worth of life insurance provides an income of $14,000 a year. Using both principal and 7 percent interest, $148,000 worth of insurance will provide $14,000 a year for 20 years; $200,000 worth would yield nearly $19,000 annually.

For a doctor with a young wife and children, it's generally more realistic to adopt a principal-plus-interest plan that terminates when all the children have finished school. Presumably, by that time the widow will have remarried or gone to work.

Provision for your family's living expenses is the key factor in your insurance program. With that out of the way, calculating the lump sums necessary to meet other family needs is relatively easy.

BOX 5B
Estimating your life insurance needs

With this worksheet you can determine roughly the amount required for your family to maintain their current lifestyle if you die in the near future. It's a good idea to review these figures every few years and adjust your coverage to your changing circumstances.

A. Survivors' annual living expenses[1] $ _____

B. Annual Social Security survivors' benefits[1] _____

C. Net living expenses for survivors (A minus B) _____

D. Capital needed to produce amount on line C[2] _____

E. Special needs (college tuition, home mortgage, other large debts)[3] _____

F. Death expenses[1] _____

G. Total funding required (add D, E, and F) _____

H. Present funds available[4] _____

I. Life insurance needs (G minus H) _____

J. Present insurance coverage[5] _____

K. Amount of insurance to be added or dropped (difference between I and J) $ _____

[1]See discussion in this chapter.
[2]See table.
[3]Unless covered by existing policy riders (see Box 5E).
[4]Value of retirement-fund assets plus personal savings and salable investments.
[5]Including group insurance through your professional corporation, etc.

Assumed investment yield	To find capital needed (Line D), multiply Line C by factor shown in column below, depending on how long income is required:				
	10 years	15 years	20 years	25 years	30 years
6%	7.8	10.3	12.2	13.6	14.6
7	7.5	9.7	11.3	12.5	13.3
8	7.2	9.2	10.6	11.5	12.2
9	7.0	8.8	10.0	10.7	11.2
10	6.8	8.4	9.4	10.0	10.4
12	6.3	7.6	8.4	8.8	9.0
15	5.8	6.7	7.2	7.4	7.6

Estate planning strategies for physicians

BOX 5C
Estimating short-term disability income needs

Bear in mind that a disability could change the amount you normally spend for some items. For example, your insurance costs might be reduced by waiver-of-premium clauses; car and entertainment outlays might decline; lower earnings would reduce your income taxes. Remember, too, that disability insurance benefits are tax free if you paid the policy premiums, but not if your corporation paid them.

Type of expense	Estimated monthly amount
Rent or mortgage payments	$ _____
Utilities	_____
Home maintenance	_____
Property taxes	_____
Property insurance	_____
Life insurance	_____
Disability insurance	_____
Auto insurance	_____
Auto payments and maintenance	_____
Entertainment, hobbies	_____
Food	_____
Clothing	_____
Debt reduction	_____
Children's education	_____
Charity	_____
Medical and dental	_____
Federal and state income taxes	_____
Other	_____
Total expenses	$ _____

Benefits depend on such factors as your age, how long you've been covered by Social Security, and how much retirement-income credit you've accumulated by the time you die or become disabled. The benefits shown are averages; the maximum could exceed $16,000 a year in some cases, and all benefits are subject to adjustment for inflation in the future.

Children under 18 are eligible for benefits due to your death or disability; so is your spouse while caring for a child under 16 or (as your survivor) after age 60. However, there's a ceiling on total family benefits when more than two persons are eligible.

Keep in mind that, to be covered, a disability must prevent you from doing "substantial gainful work" for at least 12 months; payments start after the fifth month. If you become eligible for retirement benefits while disabled, you'll get whichever type is higher.

Beneficiaries	Monthly benefit	Annual benefit
Young survivor family	$950	$11,400
Widowed spouse (60 or older)	400	4,800
Disabled worker alone	450	5,400
Disabled worker and family	875	10,500

Source: Social Security Administration.

Children's college fund

The younger your children are when you die, the more time there will be for interest to accumulate on the money set aside for their college education. But while that fund is growing, college expenses will be rising, too. To be on the safe side, better allow for a college fund of at least $40,000 for each of your children, regardless of present age. That way, whether a child starts college next year or 10 years from now, he or she will likely have enough to make it through four years.

Mortgage and other large debts

You'll want to relieve your surviving spouse of the burden of paying off any mortgage or other large fixed expenses you now have. So enter the total amount of those obligations on the worksheet.

Death expenses

Part of your estate will go to pay the expenses of your last illness, funeral costs, minor outstanding obligations, executor's fees, and other administrative costs. To provide for them and other unforeseeable contingencies, it's wise to add 5 percent to the total of the three preceeding categories (family living, college, and other large expenses). You may need to increase that added amount to allow for inheritance taxes (see Chapter 2).

From the grand total, subtract the value of your savings and investments. The difference is the amount of insurance you need to provide for your family. Next, subtract the value of the insurance coverage you now have. The result is the amount of coverage you should add. If the figure seems beyond your means, group insurance available to you may lower the cost of premiums.

Review your coverage periodically

The life insurance program you adopted in your early practice years may well have become inadequate because of additions to your family, the assumption of large mortgages and other debts, the incorporation of your practice, and the erosive effects of inflation. On the other hand, with the mortgage paid off and the children grown, less coverage may be required. The need for life insurance also depends on the amount of other assets you have accumulated. All this means that a careful review of your insurance needs and current policies is in order as time passes.

BOX 5E
Policy riders to consider

A family protection rider to a life insurance policy covers a stated number of years from the policy's inception date and pays specific amounts monthly in addition to the face value of the policy. A mortgage rider simply takes over the mortgage payments. The longer you live, the smaller the number of payments the insurance company has to make on these riders, which are, in reality, "reducing-term" policies. They're a bargain if you die in the early years of the policy, but in later years you're shelling out the same amount of premium for coverage that's disappearing.

A waiver of premium rider is usually a good investment. Then if you as policyholder become disabled, your life insurance remains in force without any further payment of premiums during the period of your disability. If the policy is the whole-life type, the cash values continue to mount even though the premiums are waived.

DROPPING EXCESS COVERAGE

The time will probably come when your insurance coverage is greater than your needs, either because your family financial obligations have diminished or because your other assets have grown substantially since you bought your policies. Here are some points to consider before you take action to trim your excess coverage:

□ Your heirs may need cash even if your estate is ample and final expenses and taxes are relatively light. If you own real estate or other nonliquid assets that you wouldn't want your heirs to have to sell at a time not of their choosing, it may be wise to protect against that eventuality by keeping your life insurance in force. (Estate liquidity problems are discussed in greater detail in Chapter 7.)

□ Don't overlook the death benefits in your retirement plan when assessing the need for life insurance in the later years of your practice. If you started early and made your plan contributions regularly, their value may well make cashing in your policies a good financial option.

□ If you do decide to scale down insurance coverage, it's usually best to drop your newest policies first, since they carry the highest cost per thousand dollars of insurance. They probably also have the highest borrowing rate. It may come in handy to retain policies that allow you to borrow at a low rate. And it may be wise at this point to borrow some of that money and put it to work at a higher rate than you have to pay for borrowing it.

Remember, your heirs don't get the death benefit *plus* the accumulated cash value; they just get the death benefit. If you can borrow the amount at 4 or 5 percent and invest at 8 or 9, you are really depriving yourself and your family by not doing so. The argument against borrowing is that your heirs will not receive the amount of the outstanding loan. It's not a strong argument in the light of interest rates that have prevailed in recent years. Almost always, the death benefit minus the loan, plus the side fund growing at a more favorable interest rate, will dramatically exceed the policy's full death benefit even after the payment of interest on the loan over the years.

□ When investing borrowed cash values, think first of assured yield and safety; this isn't money you'd want to speculate with. You might consider a single-premium deferred annuity as the investment vehicle. The interest is compounded on a tax-deferred basis and is partially protected by a guaranteed minimum yield if there is a sharp drop in interest rates. Moreover, the annuity is payable as a death benefit and can make up the gap in insurance protection caused by the amount borrowed.

□ If you have both "participating" (dividend-paying) and nonparticipating policies of some vintage, consider hanging on to those that pay dividends and cashing in the nonparticipating ones. The reason is that the size of the dividend increases over time, reducing the net cost of the policy. The quoted premium of a nonparticipating policy is always lower than that of a participating one, but in five to 10 years the net cost generally equalizes, and the participating policy gains a gradually increasing edge thereafter.

☐ Consider dropping paidup policies. If you have any endowment or 20-year-pay policies that have matured, you aren't getting much pure protection; the cash value might equal half the face amount. You could surrender the policy, take the cash, put it safely in high-quality securities like Treasury notes, and buy another policy with part of the income if you still need the protection.

Suppose you bought a $50,000, 20-year-payment policy 20 years ago, at age 30. Today you own a paidup policy with about $26,000 in cash value. Your net insurance, however, is really only $24,000 (the $50,000 face amount minus the $26,000 cash value). If you surrender the policy, invest the cash for income, and buy a term policy with a face value of $24,000 for about $700 or $800 a year, your beneficiary will still receive $50,000 when you die: $24,000 in insurance and $26,000 in savings. But that $26,000 will be earning perhaps $2,500 or more a year in pretax interest. That's enough to pay the premium on the new policy and still add substantially to your assets. If you sat with your old policy, your cash value would continue to grow, but your beneficiary would still receive only $50,000 at your death.

Keep in mind, however, that when you cash in an old policy, any cash value exceeding what you've paid in premiums is taxed as ordinary income. Say your premiums on the paidup policy totaled $27,000, reduced by $4,000 in dividends. Your net cost is $23,000, so $3,000 of the $26,000 cash value would be taxable.

ANNUITIES

An annuity is a contract with an insurance company in which you promise to deposit a certain amount of money, and the insurance company, in turn, promises to pay you an income from that deposit. With a conventional or fixed annuity, the payout will be the same month after month. That's the conservative route. With a variable annuity, the company is allowed to take more chances with the money you've given it to invest. The value of your account fluctuates, and so will the payout.

The company agrees to pay you an income starting at a set date. It may agree to keep on paying until you die (a life-only annuity) or as long as you or your spouse lives (a joint-and-survivor annuity). Or it may promise to at least repay all the principal (a refund annuity) or to make payments for a minimum number of years, typically 10, regardless of when you die. This last kind of contract, called a years-certain annuity, would pay you for life, but should you die after eight years, say, two more years of payments would be made to your beneficiary. Of course, the longer you build in guarantees for your spouse and survivors, the more expensive the contract will be (or the lower the payout). In any case, if you die before the payout period commences, your beneficiary will receive at least the amount of principal you had put in.

If you come to the age you had set for the payout to begin, you don't have to start realizing the income right away. You can let it ride to continue compounding the way it has been. Or you can probably withdraw just the original principal, tax-free, allowing the accumulated interest to keep on earning more for you and delaying the day on which any of the investment return will become taxable.

Note that if you withdraw funds *before* the annuity starting date, as some contracts permit, the withdrawals may be treated as taxable income to the extent that the cash value of the annuity exceeds the premiums paid. (Earnings on annuity investments made prior to August 14, 1982, aren't subject to this rule.) A loan under the contract will also be treated as a cash withdrawal for income tax purposes. You might even have to pay a 5 percent penalty if you make a premature withdrawal from an annuity contract that is less than 10 years old, though the penalty won't apply if you've reached age $59\frac{1}{2}$ or have become disabled.

Assuming you keep the annuity until it matures when you're 65, you might expect to collect about $1,025 a month from a $100,000 annuity if you choose the life-only option; $950 with 10 years certain; or $825 with 20 years certain. With the joint-and-survivor option (both annuitants aged 65 at maturity), the amount you collect while you both live depends on the percentage you want the survivor to have: $950 a month if the survivor is to get half ($475); $850 if the survivor gets two-thirds ($567); $750 if the survivor gets 100 percent (also $750). But payouts vary widely from company to company, so comparison-shop before you sign up.

DISABILITY INSURANCE

Serious illnesses and accidents can derail any doctor's financial program. Even something as minor as a broken ankle can be a severe blow if he has neglected to buy adequate insurance and lacks someone to cover his practice.

Your need for income during a disability is predicated on your projected living expenses (see the worksheet in Box 5C). Don't try to duplicate 100 percent of your current income. A good rule of thumb suggested by respected insurance advisers is to aim at covering about half of your pretax income by insurance, Social Security, and other benefits. Specifying a reasonably long waiting period before the insurance payments are to begin allows you to buy higher amounts, longer-lasting coverage, and policies with the most desirable insuring clauses.

Look first for policies that are noncancelable and guaranteed renewable. This means that, no matter what happens to your health, the insurance company can't cancel the policy or change its premium structure so long as you pay your premiums. Some noncancelable policies call for a stepup of premiums at later ages. That's not optimum, but still highly acceptable.

The definition of disability in the policy is equally important. Preferably you should be entitled to benefits if you can't perform your specialty or can't earn your previous level of income in your specialty. Next best is a policy that pays benefits for a given length of time (often two years) if you are unable to perform your occupation, and thereafter pays if you can't perform any occupation for which your education, training, or experience qualifies you. Thus, in the third year of disability, a surgeon with an injured hand would lose coverage if he could do consulting work or teach in medical school.

Be firm in demanding a clear, unequivocal explanation of the definition of disability in any policy you're considering. Also be wary of these fine-print take-aways:

☐ A clause giving the insurance company the right to review your earnings level when the disability occurs.

☐ A clause giving the company the right to hold off paying benefits, even after the end of the waiting period, until all practice income has stopped, including receipts from outstanding accounts or salary from your professional corporation.

☐ A policy benefit that is expressed as a percentage of earnings, but that doesn't count professional-corporation bonuses as earnings.

☐ A policy whose benefits are reduced should you receive pension-plan benefits.

If you must compromise, stint on the size of benefits rather than their duration. It's better to be a few hundred dollars a month short of the ideal in the earlier years of a disability than to run out entirely in later years.

Group insurance available through your medical society or other professional association provides the most coverage for the lowest premium. But be mindful that even "noncancelable" group policies can be canceled if the insurer decides to drop the group. So use them to top up your coverage but rely on individual policies for bedrock insurance.

After your home mortgage is paid off and the children are grown, you're likely to need less disability-income protection. Use the worksheet in Box 5C to help you determine any excess. Don't neglect to include in your calculations the estimated monthly payout of your retirement plan in the event of disability. By this time, it could be a handsome amount.

If you feel you can safely discontinue some disability coverage, first drop policies that tie benefits to a set percentage of earnings. The maximum benefits of such policies will begin to decline as you wind down your practice, but the premiums won't. Next drop policies that the company can cancel or that have unattractive disability definitions. Only if you have nothing but noncancelable policies with favorable disability clauses should you make premium comparisons the basis for discontinuance.

BOX 5F
Estimating office overhead insurance needs

Policy benefits are limited to the expenses you actually incur, so if you simply project current expenses, you would overinsure yourself. Have your bookkeeper list your normal expenses; then try to anticipate what would happen if you weren't able to practice for an extended period. Consider whether you would need a full complement of personnel and for how long, and whether outlays for items like laundry would continue at current levels. Omit expense items that overhead insurance won't cover—e.g., mortgage principal payments, salaries of substitute physicians, cost of drugs and equipment.

Type of expense	Normal monthly amount	Estimated monthly amount if disabled
Office rent or mortgage interest and taxes	$ _____	$ _____
Office payroll	_____	_____
Interest on loans for professional purposes	_____	_____
Heat and utilities	_____	_____
Telephone answering service	_____	_____
Professional services (accounting, etc.)	_____	_____
Building maintenance	_____	_____
Office insurance premiums	_____	_____
Professional car expenses	_____	_____
Depreciation of furniture and equipment	_____	_____
Professional dues	_____	_____
Laundry	_____	_____
Stationery and postage	_____	_____
Other	_____	_____
Total expenses	$ _____	$ _____

Estate planning strategies for physicians

Note: If you're in solo practice or in an unincorporated partnership, office overhead insurance may be worth considering as an adjunct to disability coverage (see Box 5F).

MINIMIZING TAXES ON POLICY PROCEEDS

Life insurance policies usually offer a choice between lump-sum payment of the proceeds and various installment options. It's wiser to leave the choice to your beneficiary, if competent, rather than making it yourself. A lump-sum payout is generally exempt from federal income tax, but installment payouts may be partially taxable.

For example, if the beneficiary of a $100,000 policy chooses to take the proceeds in 10 annual installments of $15,000, then $5,000 of each installment is taxable as interest. However, if the beneficiary is your spouse, only $4,000 would be taxed because there's a $1,000 yearly interest exclusion for a widow or widower. The exclusion doesn't apply, though, if the proceeds remain with the insurance company under an "interest only" option instead of being paid out in installments. In that case, all the interest earned would be taxable.

While income taxes won't ordinarily reduce the proceeds your beneficiaries receive, estate taxes might, so you have to take that possibility into account in your insurance planning. But there is no immediate federal tax problem if your spouse is the beneficiary, since she inherits everything tax-free under the law passed in 1981.

Suppose the amount of insurance you now carry was determined before then and included an allowance for estate taxes. Should you reduce your coverage accordingly?

Let's assume that you have $200,000 of life insurance and $400,000 of other assets, all going to your spouse. Under the old law, she would have received less than $560,000 after taxes. With the present unlimited marital deduction, she will get the full $600,000. If you believe that your spouse should be content with $560,000, you would drop about $40,000 worth of coverage and save about 20 percent on the premiums. But there's an argument for keeping the $40,000 coverage as extra protection against inflation.

A married couple may not need insurance to cover estate taxes when the first one dies. But the tax bite could become much sharper at the second death, because the marital deduction won't apply then. A policy that pays off only after both you and your spouse die might be the answer. The premiums would be lower than those for a policy covering either of you alone. Even so, it may not be worth the cost unless you're pretty sure your future heirs will need the protection.

Estate taxes also bear on another life insurance question: Who should own your policy? If *you* do, the proceeds will be part of your estate when you

If you transfer ownership of a policy, its cash value, if any, is a gift. When the new owner is your spouse, there's no tax since the unlimited marital deduction applies. You can claim the $10,000 annual exclusion ($20,000 if your spouse consents) on a policy gift to a person other than your spouse. If you continue to pay the premiums, the annual exclusion applies to them as well.

What if your spouse exercises ownership rights and names someone else — your child, say — as beneficiary? When the child collects the proceeds at your death, they count as a gift taxable to your spouse, though she can claim a $10,000 exclusion — not $20,000, because you're no longer alive to join in. If there are several beneficiaries, she can claim a $10,000 exclusion for each. However, it's usually preferable for your spouse to be beneficiary; she can then distribute the proceeds to the children over a number of years, claiming the annual exclusion for each separate gift.

As discussed in this chapter, transferring policy ownership to a trust may be a more effective way to keep insurance proceeds out of your and your spouse's estates. But be aware that the annual exclusion normally can't be claimed either on the cash-value gift to the trust or on subsequent premiums you continue to pay directly. If the trustee pays the premiums with income from assets you've contributed to the trust, the premiums aren't subject to gift tax, but the assets are.

Of course, the unified gift/estate tax credit is applicable to insurance gifts. If the non-insurance portion of your estate isn't large enough to use up most of your (and your spouse's) credit, insurance gift taxes should not be a significant problem. If they are, your estate-planning attorney can suggest ways to make insurance gifts that will hold down or avoid the taxes.

If transferring policy ownership is desirable in your situation, don't procrastinate. Should you die less than three years after giving a policy away, the proceeds will be included in your estate regardless of who owns the policy at your death.

---

die. One way to avoid that is by making your beneficiary the owner of the policy. There's no purpose in doing that if your spouse is the beneficiary; whether you or she owns the policy, she won't be taxed on the proceeds. But they could increase the size of *her* estate.*

If you want to completely avoid an estate tax bite on your insurance, you'll have to get it out of your spouse's estate as well as your own. The best way to do that is to set up a trust during your lifetime, turn your policies over to the trustee—who should not be you or your spouse—and continue to pay premiums on them. At your death, the proceeds go to the trustee, who invests or distributes them in accordance with the terms of the trust. Any gift tax involved is likely to be far less than the estate tax saving on the proceeds (see Box 5G).

---

*In a community-property state, if premiums are paid from common funds, your spouse owns half the policy, which means that half the cash value will be in her estate if she dies first. There may also be a problem if the policy is transferred to a trust in which she has a life interest.

You could instead turn over securities to the trustee and have him use the dividends to pay the insurance premiums. This arrangement avoids estate taxes not only on the insurance proceeds but also on the securities themselves. It does leave you liable for income tax on the dividends used to pay the insurance premiums, because the insurance is on your life. (In addition, there may be a gift tax.)

You can direct that, after your death, the trustee is to pay your spouse the income from the insurance proceeds, and even part of the principal, with the rest going to the children at her death. This bypass arrangement will keep the proceeds out of your spouse's estate.

Although you can't control or revoke the trust, you can build a good deal of flexibility into it at the start. For instance, you might authorize the trustee, if you become disabled, to pay out the insurance cash value as income to your spouse while you're alive. You could give the trustee broad discretion to make growth investments with some of the insurance money after your death, if it isn't all needed to provide income for your family.

You can't, however, direct the trustee to pay estate taxes or debts with the insurance proceeds. That would put them right back in your estate. What you can do is give him discretion to purchase estate assets or lend the estate money to overcome a temporary cash shortage.

If an insurance trust seems suitable for you but you're hesitant about finally committing yourself, you can arrange for the trust to be revocable initially. Later on, you can make it irrevocable if it works to your satisfaction, or call the whole thing off if it doesn't. (But beware of the three-year rule discussed in Box 5G.)

If your main concern is providing estate management for your heirs, your attorney may suggest having *all* your assets go into the insurance trust at your death. Such a "pour-over" arrangement can help unify the management of your estate by putting everything in the hands of a trustee rather than splitting control between executor and trustee.

For a discussion of how state inheritance taxes may affect your insurance planning, see Chapter 2.

6

Make your pension fund the keystone

A tax-sheltered pension fund is the keystone of the typical doctor's financial program and deserves commensurate attention in estate planning.

Present law makes few distinctions between the retirement plans set up by unincorporated doctors (usually called "Keogh plans") and those of professional corporations. Nearly all MDs' plans fit into one of two broad categories. More common are plans in which contributions are based on a percentage of income from practice. These are known as defined-contribution plans. The law now generally permits doctors with such plans to contribute up to 25 percent of salary (including bonuses) if incorporated, or 25 percent of earned practice income if unincorporated. The terms "salary" and "earned practice income" are equivalent—each equals practice net, minus plan contributions for yourself.

For example, a solo incorporated MD netting $100,000 after expenses could pay himself a salary of $80,000 and contribute $20,000. So could an unincorporated doctor netting $100,000. Looked at another way, either MD is allowed to contribute 20 percent of his $100,000 practice net. When the unincorporated doctor contributes $20,000, he's left with earned practice income of $80,000; the incorporated MD is left with $80,000 of salary. For simplicity, from here on we'll say "salary" whether you're incorporated or not.

The other main retirement-plan category is the defined-benefit plan, so called because you first decide on the amount of annual benefit to be paid in retirement. The size of the annual contributions is based on the benefit goal and is not directly affected by what you earn from year to year. The advantages and disadvantages of defined-benefit plans in relation to defined-contribution plans will be detailed later.

All pension plans offer these tax advantages:

☐ Because every dollar you put in reduces your current tax bill, you can invest more than you could on your own without reducing spendable income.

☐ Income and capital gains earned by a retirement fund aren't taxed currently. That allows a more rapid buildup, since the fund's entire income is available for reinvestment.

☐ Although the money will be taxed when you get it later on, by then you may be in a lower bracket and pay less. If the money is paid out in a lump sum, the tax is computed at special favorable rates.

What are the major factors in determining the type of plan to choose? One consideration is how much you want to put away. (Generally, a defined-benefit plan will allow you to make larger contributions.) Equally important is the size of the payroll and the ages of your office assistants. If you don't have much office help, it won't matter what you do. If you have a large staff, though, you may have to select a plan that will let you put away less for the assistants—especially if they're younger than you.

DEFINED-CONTRIBUTION PLANS

Early in your career, your best bet is likely to be a defined-contribution plan, in which you contribute a percentage of your salary. You can do this with a "money-purchase" plan, where the percentage is fixed; with a profit-sharing plan, which allows you to vary the percentage from year to year; or with a combination of both. This arrangement requires no complicated formulas to figure out the contributions for you and the staff.

Let's say your annual salary is $80,000 and you have a money-purchase plan that calls for a contribution of 10 percent. The sum of $8,000 goes into your retirement plan annually. Then, if you also have a profit-sharing plan, you can put away an additional amount up to 15 percent, or $12,000. You'd normally contribute the same percentage for your eligible employees.

The annual ceiling on total tax-deductible contributions to money-purchase and profit-sharing plans is 25 percent of salary, but not more than $30,000. (The dollar limit will be adjusted in the future to keep pace with inflation.) You can build up your retirement fund even more by making a voluntary (non-tax-deductible) contribution, up to 6 percent of your salary—more in some cases. You can also contribute to an IRA.

Within those limits, you can tailor the defined-contribution plan to your specific needs. You can have a money-purchase plan alone and contribute any amount up to the overall limit. However, you must fix the percentage in advance, so it will apply in lean years as well as in fat ones. Against that disadvantage, you'll get the advantage of saving administrative costs by having only one plan.

You can opt for a profit-sharing plan alone and have complete flexibility over the amount you contribute, but there's a disadvantage. The maximum annual contribution to this type of plan can't exceed 15 percent of your pay.

With a combination of the two plans, you can have flexibility plus the right to contribute the tax-deductible maximum. The money-purchase contribution can be set at, say, 10 percent of salary. Then each year you can decide how much more—from zero up to 15 percent—you want to put into your profit-sharing plan. In exchange for that flexibility, you'll have to pay the cost of running two plans.

DEFINED-BENEFIT PLANS

Contributions to this type of plan depend on the annual retirement pension you'd like to have. This can be a set dollar figure or a percentage of your preretirement salary. There are two limitations on the size of the pension you can aim for. It must not be more than 100 percent of your average salary during your three highest consecutive working years. Nor can your pension exceed $90,000 annually if you pick a retirement age of 62 to 65. The dollar limit is lower if retirement is to begin before 62, higher if later than 65. In the future, the dollar limits will be adjusted for inflation.

Note that what's limited is the pension figure, *not* the annual contributions. An actuary must compute how much you have to put away each year to accumulate the fund you'll need at retirement to pay the benefit you want. In the calculations, the actuary has to make assumptions about such matters as the rate of investment return on plan funds both before and after retirement, your life expectancy, and possibly the rate of inflation. These assumptions must be reasonable, but the actuary has considerable leeway, especially if there are many years to go before your retirement.

Obviously, if the actuary assumes low investment return rates, you'll need a bigger fund to meet your goal, calling for larger annual contributions. To some extent, therefore, the size of the contributions can be shaped to your financial situation. However, the actuary must review the plan annually and certify that it's on track. If it's over- or underfunded because actual rates of return have varied too greatly from expectations, or for other reasons, then subsequent contributions must be adjusted up or down accordingly.

In most cases, a defined-benefit plan will permit you to make larger tax-deductible contributions than you could with a defined-contribution plan. Take a doctor at age 50 with an annual net of $80,000. The most he's allowed to put into a defined-contribution plan is $16,000. But if he wants to contribute $24,000 a year, leaving him a salary of $56,000, he can do that with a defined-benefit plan. That would give him an annual retirement benefit of roughly $34,000. By taking an even lower salary, the doctor could increase the annual tax-deductible contribution further. But the pension benefit for all eligible employees would have to be the same percentage of salary as for him, and the contributions he makes for them would be correspondingly higher.

Defined-benefit plans are not suitable for every doctor. The younger you are, the more time there is to build your fund, so the less you're allowed to set aside each year. If the doctor in the above example were 35 instead of 50, he could probably contribute more to a conventional defined-contribution plan.

Even a young MD might do well with a defined-benefit plan by choosing a lower retirement age. The law permits you to go as low as 55. A 32-year-old doctor with a salary of $75,000 could put perhaps $22,000 a year in a defined-benefit plan for retirement at age 55. (He could put only $18,750 in a defined-contribution plan, since he'd be limited to 25 percent of salary.) Once he reached age 55, his pension would be fully funded, so his contributions would have to stop. But he could leave the accumulated assets intact and let the tax-sheltered earnings increase his retirement benefit.

What if you choose a defined-benefit plan and later find you can't afford the contributions required, even with favorable actuarial assumptions? At any time, it's possible to revise the plan and reduce your contributions. In that event, part of the money you've put in for yourself and your employees would become 100 percent vested, and your employees would have the right to take their money if they left.

Whatever the tax advantages of setting up a defined-benefit plan to enrich the contributions in your retirement fund, remember that your take-home pay will drop. If that's going to strap you financially or interfere with your other commitments, like paying your children's college expenses, you may not be able to afford the plan. If you're incorporated, your decision may be influenced by the fact that you can borrow plan funds, within limits and under strict repayment rules; unincorporated doctors are *not* allowed to borrow from their plans.

If you want to adopt a defined-benefit plan but already have a defined-contribution plan, you can "freeze" it. That is, you stop contributing to it, but the assets continue to earn tax-deferred income until you retire. However, the actuary must take those frozen assets into account in figuring how much you're allowed to accumulate in your defined-benefit plan.

An alternative is to have a combination plan—a defined-contribution plan and a defined-benefit plan as well. Total benefits under the two plans are usually 25 percent higher than the single-plan limit, provided you—and other doctor-participants—don't get more than 90 percent of plan benefits.

BENEFIT FORMULAS

The formula used for calculating *your* pension benefits must also be used for *your employees*. As a rule, that means the percentage of salary contributed will be identical for all. But not always.

BOX 6A
How big a defined-benefit plan you can have

You can set a maximum pension benefit equal to 100 percent of your salary, based on a three year average. It's usually desirable to assume that your pension is to be fully funded at age 62, even if you may not retire that soon. The upper table shows, for example, that a doctor who starts a pension plan at age 45 can contribute up to 30 percent of practice net annually. If the net is $100,000, you can make a $30,000 contribution; your "salary" will be $70,000 and so will your annual pension at age 62. Note that the contribution equals 43 percent of the salary.

Suppose you pay your 30-year-old assistant a $10,000 salary. The lower table shows that you'd have to contribute only 13 percent of it, or $1,300, to fund a $10,000 annual pension for her. As you can see, the contributions required for older employees could be considerably higher. The contributions would be reduced if your pension-benefit goal were less than 100 percent of salary.

The percentages shown here may vary from year to year due to forfeitures, fluctuations in plan earnings, and other factors. Higher initial percentages are possible if more aggressive actuarial assumptions are used. The IRS might not challenge them while the fund is building up, but it can apply strict standards when the time comes to distribute the money. If the IRS finds there's too much in the fund then, you could face a costly day of reckoning.

Your age when plan starts	Percent of net you can contribute[1]
35	16%
40	22
45	30
50	42
55	47[2]

Employee's age	Percent of salary to be contributed[1]
25	9%
30	13
35	19
40	28
45	43
50	71
55	87[2]

[1] To fund joint-and-survivor annuity (50 percent annuity for survivor) starting at age 62. Assumed plan earnings rate: 6 percent.
[2] Pension starts at age 65.

Estate planning strategies for physicians

Under some circumstances, you can end up contributing a greater percentage of salary for your employees than you do for yourself. That's because in determining the contribution percentage for your employees, only the first $200,000 of your salary counts. If you net $250,000, for instance, your maximum $30,000 contribution would be only 13.6 percent of the $220,000 salary. But you'd have to contribute 15 percent (your $30,000 contribution divided by $200,000) of your employees' salaries.

Defined-benefit plans are another case in point. In such plans, the contribution required for each participant depends not only on salary but also on age. Suppose a doctor's plan calls for a pension at age 62 equal to 100 percent of salary. If he and his assistant are the same age—45, say—the annual contribution ratio will be about the same for both: roughly 43 percent of salary. But if the assistant is only 30, the ratio drops to 13 percent for her (see Box 6A).

Another permissible way to vary contributions in a defined-benefit plan is by using a formula that gives credit for prior service. If you've been in practice, say, 15 years when you adopt the plan, you could start off with a higher accrued benefit than an assistant who's been with you for 10 years. Suppose each year of service is worth 3 percent of salary. The first-year contributions would be based on a pension of 45 percent of salary for you, but only 30 percent for your assistant.

Caution: By law, a defined-benefit plan must provide a payout of at least 2 percent of salary for every employee for each year of service, up to a maximum of 20 percent. So if a nurse worked for you for 10 years and was paid an average of $15,000, the plan must provide her with at least $3,000 a year at retirement. (If the employee is also covered by a defined-contribution plan, this rule may not apply.)

RETIREMENT-PLAN LIFE INSURANCE

There are two ways to buy life insurance coverage through a retirement plan:

(1) The trustee can use part of the plan contributions for insurance. That's known as a "split-funded" plan, because the assets are split between insurance and investments.

(2) The trustee can buy combined annuity and life insurance contracts. That's known as an "insured" plan, because all the assets are invested in insurance.

You can use up to one-half of the contributions in a defined-contribution plan to purchase life insurance. In a defined-benefit plan, the limit is placed on the face value of the policy—100 times the monthly retirement benefit.

These days, almost nobody but a life insurance salesman would recommend buying life insurance with retirement-plan funds except in unusual circumstances. Term premiums aren't tax deductible at all, and even whole-life premiums are partially taxable as current income. What's more, the value of the benefits is included in your estate, and payments to your beneficiary are taxable income.

Because the interest you can get on the money in your retirement plan compounds tax-free, it makes sense to put as much of the assets directly to work as possible and not divert the money into insurance. If you need insurance coverage, buy it outside of the plan.

If you were to put, say, $10,000 a year into a Keogh plan and use $1,000 of it to pay a term premium, you could tax-deduct only $9,000. In the 38 percent bracket, this costs you $380 in tax savings. Now suppose you're also able to salt away $1,000 a year outside your plan. If you use *that* money to pay for the insurance, you'll still be putting $10,000 annually into your Keogh. Not only will you get the full tax saving, but you'll also have $10,000, rather than $9,000, earning tax-deferred, compound interest for you.

There's another disadvantage to buying life insurance through your retirement plan if you have a high personnel turnover. As you know, most of the first years' premiums are used to pay commissions; cash value builds up later. Thus, a lot of the money that employees forfeit if they leave before they're vested winds up in the hands of the insurance company or salesman instead of benefiting the remaining plan participants.

PENSION PAYOUT OPTIONS

Your options are limited on when you can take your pension funds out. Unless disabled, you can't start withdrawing money from your plan until you're 59½, and you *must* start when you reach 70½.

Almost as important as building up your retirement fund is understanding the various payout options that are open to you and deciding *how* to take the money out. If the payout isn't planned properly, taxes could leave you with less than you expected.

All of the money in your pension account is taxable when it's paid out, except voluntary (nondeductible) contributions you have made to the plan. However, if you withdraw the entire amount in one tax year, it's eligible for special 10-year tax averaging. Here's how that deferment strategy can work to your advantage:

The total payout is divided by 10, and the tax a single person would pay on that amount (ignoring other income) is multiplied by 10. The resulting amount is your tax on the fund payout. (Single-person rates apply even if you're married and file a joint return.) Since this income isn't added to your other income, it doesn't boost your regular tax bracket. Furthermore, if you made any contributions before 1974, you can elect capital-gains treatment on part of the payout.

BOX 6B
Tax rates on lump-sum benefits

When pension benefits are taken as a lump sum, the special 10-year averaging method described in the text can be used to figure the tax. The effective tax rates shown in the table apply regardless of the amount of other taxable income you have in the year of distribution.

Lump-sum distribution	Effective tax rate*
$ 50,000	12%
100,000	15
150,000	17
200,000	19
250,000	21
300,000	23
400,000	26
500,000	29
600,000	32
700,000	34
800,000	36
900,000	37
1,000,000	39

*Based on 1985 tax schedule.

For example, the tax on a $400,000 lump-sum payout would come to less than $105,000 with 10-year averaging (see Box 6B). That would save you more than $95,000 if your other income put you in the 50 percent bracket. But if your top bracket in retirement figures to be considerably lower, you might do better to spread a hefty payout over a number of years, unless you happen to need a large sum for some immediate purpose.

Paying the tax on a lump-sum distribution all at once reduces the amount of money working for you. By taking your pension in installments from the pension trust, you draw down the principal only gradually, and the earnings on it continue to compound tax-free.

One thing to remember about installments: The law requires that they be big enough so that the payout can be completed within your life expectancy, or your own and your spouse's joint expectancy. A man retiring at 65, for example, is expected to live some 15 years; a woman, a little more than 18; and one member of a couple, both 65, about 22 years (see Box 6C).

Another alternative, if you don't need the pension money in the early years of retirement, is to withdraw it from your pension account and put it into an IRA within 60 days. Then you can take out money as needed and pay taxes

Here's how long the IRS assumes lifetime annuities are likely to run.

Age	Male life expectancy	Female life expectancy	Joint life expectancy*
61	18 years	21 years	25 years
62	17	20	24
63	16	20	24
64	16	19	23
65	15	18	22
66	14	18	21
67	14	17	21
68	13	16	20
69	13	16	19
70	12	15	18

*Assuming both are the same age. If the female is two or three years younger, add one or two years.

only on that amount. What's left still compounds tax-free. You must start withdrawals from the IRA no later than age 70½, and they must be large enough to exhaust the fund within your (and your spouse's) life expectancy.

Two problems with a rollover IRA: You lose the right to get capital-gains treatment for contributions made before 1974, and you lose the 10-year averaging option. But if you have any self-employment income after retirement from the practice, you can set up a new Keogh plan and roll your IRA over into it one year after you've retired (not before that). Once in the Keogh plan, you regain the option of 10-year averaging.

Still another option is to take the payout from your retirement plan in the form of an annuity payable as long as you live or as long as either you or your spouse lives. In general, the law requires a pension plan to provide a joint-and-survivor retirement annuity, as well as a preretirement annuity for your surviving spouse in case you die in harness. With your spouse's consent, you can elect not to take the payout in annuity form if you want greater control over your money and the way it's invested. (For more on annuities, see Chapter 5.)

Your plan should permit you to choose any of the above options. In addition, it should contain a clause allowing "any other payout option acceptable to the trustees and not in violation of law or regulations." This will allow you the best possible choice when you finally do retire, even if it's something not available today. But don't think this permits you to be vague about the foregoing options. See to it that they're specifically written into your plan.

The idea is to keep yourself from being boxed in when you retire. If that's a number of years away, you'll know better then how you want to take your money than you do at present. What you should do now is make sure all the options are there.

RETIREMENT BENEFITS FOR YOUR HEIRS

You may well live long enough to use up a good portion of your retirement benefits, but you should still be concerned about what happens to them after your death. If your plan has been in effect for some years, the provisions you've made should be reviewed in the light of subsequent changes in the law, as well as the increased size of your pension assets.

Chances are you can look forward to a pension fund in the high six figures or even more (see Box 6D). If you die before retirement, the value of the fund will be subject to estate tax. (If payable in installments or as an annuity, the tax will be based on the "present value" of the future payments—see Appendix 3.) Of course, if your spouse is the beneficiary, she'll get the money tax-free, thanks to the marital deduction. But piled on top of what else you're leaving her, it could result in money management problems during her lifetime and high estate taxes at her death.

There's also an income tax problem to consider. Whether your spouse (or other beneficiary) inherits your pension as a lump sum, installments, or annuity, the money is taxable income when received, just as it would have been if you'd lived to collect it. Normally, any estate tax paid on such income—known as "income in respect of a decedent"—can be deducted for income tax purposes. If your spouse is the pension beneficiary, however, she can't claim that deduction because the pension came to her free of estate tax. So if the money passes through *her* estate on its way to your children, it may be taxed both as income during her lifetime and as a legacy at her death, with no offsetting deduction.

Instead of your spouse, you could name your children or, more likely, their trust as pension beneficiary, or even make your wife the trust joint beneficiary. Since there are several variables involved, it may not be possible to predict what disposition would yield the best results years from now. The wisest course might be to let your spouse or executor make the choice if and when the time comes. As explained in Chapter 2, this can be done via either a disclaimer or a Q-TIP trust. With the former, the pension plan document names your spouse as beneficiary but allows her to disclaim part or all of the pension in favor of another beneficiary. With a Q-TIP, it is designated as pension beneficiary, and your executor makes the appropriate allocations.

Whoever the pension beneficiary or beneficiaries may be, they can elect to use 10-year averaging to determine the income tax if the pension is taken in a lump sum. Your plan document should make this option, as well as the other payout alternatives described previously, available to your beneficiaries, so that the most desirable one can be selected.

Make your pension fund the keystone

BOX 6D
How big a pension fund at retirement?

Use this worksheet to estimate the amount you'll have in your plan when you retire, assuming your annual contributions and investment return remain at present levels. The sample figures are for a 45-year-old doctor whose retirement date is 20 years off. The $15,000 contribution this year will bring his stake in the plan to $85,000 at year-end. Plan investments are yielding 8 percent.

	Sample figures	Your figures
A. Size of fund at year-end	$ 85,000	$ _____
B. Compounding factor from Table 1	4.66	_____
C. Value of present fund at retirement (A × B)	396,100	_____
D. Annual contribution	15,000	_____
E. Compounding factor from Table 2	45.76	_____
F. Value of future contributions (D × E)	686,400	_____
G. Total value of fund at retirement (C + F)	$1,082,500	_____

Table 1—Compounding factor for Line B

Years to retirement	Annual yield						
	6%	7%	8%	9%	10%	12%	15%
1	1.06	1.07	1.08	1.09	1.10	1.12	1.15
2	1.12	1.14	1.17	1.19	1.21	1.25	1.32
3	1.19	1.23	1.26	1.30	1.33	1.40	1.52
4	1.26	1.31	1.36	1.41	1.46	1.57	1.75
5	1.34	1.40	1.47	1.54	1.61	1.76	2.01
6	1.42	1.50	1.59	1.68	1.77	1.97	2.31
7	1.50	1.61	1.71	1.83	1.95	2.21	2.66
8	1.59	1.72	1.85	1.99	2.14	2.48	3.06
9	1.69	1.84	2.00	2.17	2.36	2.77	3.52
10	1.79	1.97	2.16	2.37	2.59	3.10	4.05
15	2.40	2.76	3.17	3.64	4.18	5.47	8.14
20	3.21	3.87	4.66	5.60	6.73	9.65	16.37
25	4.29	5.43	6.85	8.62	10.83	17.00	32.92
30	5.74	7.61	10.06	13.27	17.45	29.96	66.21

Estate planning strategies for physicians

Table 2 — Compounding factor for Line E

Number of years' contributions	Annual yield						
	6%	7%	8%	9%	10%	12%	15%
1	1.00	1.00	1.00	1.00	1.00	1.00	1.00
2	2.06	2.07	2.08	2.09	2.10	2.12	2.15
3	3.18	3.21	3.25	3.28	3.31	3.37	3.47
4	4.37	4.44	4.51	4.57	4.64	4.78	4.99
5	5.64	5.75	5.87	5.98	6.11	6.35	6.74
6	6.98	7.15	7.34	7.52	7.72	8.12	8.75
7	8.39	8.65	8.92	9.20	9.49	10.09	11.07
8	9.90	10.26	10.64	11.03	11.44	12.30	13.73
9	11.49	11.98	12.49	13.02	13.58	14.78	16.79
10	13.18	13.82	14.49	15.19	15.94	17.55	20.30
15	23.28	25.13	27.15	29.36	31.77	37.28	47.58
20	36.79	41.00	45.76	51.16	57.27	72.05	102.44
25	54.86	63.25	73.11	84.70	98.35	133.33	212.79
30	79.06	94.46	113.28	136.31	164.49	241.33	434.75

7

Fit your investments into the plan

What you pass on to your heirs depends not only on the amount of money you put into savings, but also on how well you invest them. So it's reasonable to assert that a program for accumulating assets deserves to be as much a part of estate planning as does one for disposing of them.

Most doctors' investment portfolios comprise three main types of holdings: common stocks and stock mutual funds; bonds and other fixed-income investments; and real estate. While income-oriented investments predominate in retirement-plan portfolios, the reverse is true in nonpension portfolios, where growth-type holdings average about three times the value of income investments.

The selection of specific investments is obviously beyond the scope of this book. Nor should it be claimed that a particular investment approach, however promising, is universally suitable. But it can be said that whatever course of action you adopt should be geared to achieving realistic objectives and based on sound investment principles. Those of major significance to the doctor investor are set forth and evaluated in the sections that follow. These options include stocks and bonds, mutual funds, and real estate. Special considerations applying to your pension-plan investments and to the postmortem estate are also discussed.

COMMON STOCKS

So-called "growth" companies typically pay small dividends, or none at all, on their stock. Instead, they reinvest their profits, believing that money spent for research or new equipment will enhance future earnings, attract new investors, and run up the market price of their stock. In theory, a growth-stock investor forgoes immediate dividends in favor of a possibly much larger future profit—a capital gain—when he eventually sells his stock. In addition, the capital gain will be taxed at more favorable rates than dividends would be.

"Income" stocks lie at the opposite end of the spectrum. They usually represent companies with limited ability to expand or increase their earnings, so they must pay high dividends to attract investors.

Investing in income stocks makes little sense for the physician whose practice income is high, except in a tax-sheltered retirement-plan portfolio. However, when untoward market conditions weaken investor confidence, growth stocks tend to drop in price much further—though they usually rebound much faster—than income stocks.

In periods of high interest rates, even growth companies must pay relatively high dividends to attract buyers for their shares. Companies that are maturing to the point where their growth rate has begun to level off tend to add a dividend "sweetener," too. International Business Machines is a classic example. In 1969, when its stock was selling at 42 times per-share earnings, its dividend was a meager 1.2 percent. More recently, however, when it sold at only 10 times earnings, it paid 5.6 percent.

Assembling a portfolio

Before you consider investing in stocks, you should have a steady—preferably growing—income, ample funds for mortgage and insurance payments, and enough savings to see you through an emergency. Investment advisers offer these suggestions for physicians who want to initiate a stock-buying program:

Take a conservative approach. Don't set any specific goals other than long-term growth of capital. Buy into large, stable companies that have good earnings records. First select the industries that seem to have the best growth ahead of them. Then choose a promising company within each industry. Invest in widely held stocks, preferably those listed on the New York Stock Exchange, to assure a ready, active market should you wish to sell.

Space out your purchases. For example, if you have $5,000 and like five stocks, buy $1,000 worth of a different stock every month for five months. That way, if the market dips a little after you buy the first stock, the next purchase may be of a stock that's about to go up. There's nothing more disconcerting to a novice than to buy stocks just before a minor market correction and see them go down.

Build on your initial investments by buying additional shares regularly—every month or every quarter. If you invest regularly in a stock, rather than trying to guess the low points, you tend to come out ahead in the long run. (This is called dollar-averaging.) Let's say you've decided to buy a stock that's selling at around $50 a share and you're putting in $500 a month. This month $500 will buy 10 shares. If the price drops to 45, say, next month you'll be able to buy 11 shares with your $500. If it goes up to 55, you'll get only nine shares, but the stock you bought in the past will have increased in value. If you buy regularly into a company whose stock is on a long-term uptrend, your cost per share over time will always average out to be less than the prevailing market price.

Diversify your holdings—but don't overdo it. No investor should hold more stocks than he can keep up with fully. An experienced, serious investor might hold 20 or 30. It's probably fair to say that half a dozen is a good number for the beginner—enough to spread the risk, yet not too many to be able to study thoroughly.

Never—well, hardly ever—have more than one-third of your holdings in any one industry, more than 20 percent in any one stock, or more than 10 stocks for every $100,000 invested.

Trade as little as possible. On the average, it costs you 1.5 percent of the stock value to buy or sell. Four trades a year more than offset most dividends. Frequent switching enriches your broker, not you.

On the other hand, don't let yourself be lulled into thinking that you have protected your money by investing in "blue chip" stocks that will take care of themselves. The market is highly susceptible to shifts in economic conditions and investor psychology. But vigilance and a rational approach to stocks can augment your net worth significantly.

Maintain a reserve fund in bank certificates of deposit, government securities, or money-market accounts. Increase these holdings when the price-earnings ratios of the stock market rise above reasonable levels. Reinvest in stocks only when there has been a substantial correction.

Review your portfolio periodically, at least every six months. Then consider selling stocks that are doing poorly and buying more shares of those that are doing well. If you sell only winners, inevitably you'll reach a point where you have a portfolio of losers.

Mutual fund alternative

Mutual funds offer small investors diversification and professional management. They're especially popular among doctors who lack the time and expertise to manage their own portfolios. Among the hundreds of mutual funds currently available, there is almost certainly one that matches your investment objective. The types of funds you'll encounter include:

□ Performance funds, which assume greater than average risks to achieve the greatest possible capital appreciation. Their portfolios often contain speculative stocks of little-known companies that the funds' analysts believe to have exceptional growth potential.

□ Growth funds, which strive for maximum appreciation consistent with safety, choosing stocks with records of sustained earnings growth.

□ Growth-with-income funds, which attempt to balance the greater risk inherent in growth stocks with lower-risk, high-income bonds or preferred stocks. Because the stock market tends to be very sensitive to interest-rate trends, these funds are a popular hedge.

□ Income funds, which invest chiefly in high-dividend-paying stocks and include a generous lacing of bonds.

Sales charges of many funds start at 8.5 percent and decline as the size of the investment goes up. There are also many so-called no-load funds that charge nothing when you buy, regardless of how modest your investment. Historically, no-load funds as a group have done better than load funds as a group in some periods, while in others the reverse has been true. So if two funds have equally good records and both match your objectives, but only one is a no-load, that could well tip the scales in its favor.

Suppose you invested $5,000 in a no-load fund that doubled its value in five years. Your investment would then be worth $10,000. If you invested the same amount in a typical load fund and it performed just as well, you would have only $9,150. If both funds doubled again in the next five years, you'd have $20,000 with the no-load, $18,300 with the load.

To buy into a load fund, you simply call your broker. To buy no-load fund shares is less convenient. Because there are no salesmen, you have to contact the fund directly. You may also have to make a larger initial investment in a no-load fund than in a load fund, although this is not always the case.

A privilege worth looking for is the right to switch from one mutual fund to another at nominal cost or no cost. This is automatic if the funds are no-loads, but it's also possible when a group or "family" of load funds is managed by the same investing firm. More than 80 such groups now offer the switching privilege.

For example, you can aim to accumulate capital in a fund whose growth record is exceptional, but which takes significant risks to achieve those gains. If market conditions change, or if you decide later that you're far enough along financially to be more interested in conservation of the capital you have accumulated or in regular income, you can switch into another fund in the same family whose stated objective coincides with yours.

Some funds offer retirement-plan services at nominal fees; others offer free estate-planning services, such as a review of your will with recommendations for you and your lawyer. A number of funds will examine and make suggestions for your portfolio of common stocks. You can also get group-rate life insurance with some plans.

Stocks in your retirement plan

While common stocks are usually acquired for nonpension portfolios in the hope of attaining capital gains, they may also provide income via dividends. Such dividend payments aren't fixed; they can go down when a company's

BOX 7A
Fixing your retirement target

How much capital will you need to get the retirement income you want? That depends on the number of years you'd like your nest egg to last and the average investment return you expect. For example, the table shows that it takes about $120,000 to provide $1,000 a month for 20 years, if your capital earns 8 percent and you're willing to use it up. To get $2,500 monthly, you'd need 2.5 times as much, or $300,000. How many years should you aim for? The life expectancy table (Box 6C) gives you a clue. The last column here shows the amounts needed if you don't want to dip into principal.

Assumed annual investment yield*	Capital required for $1,000 of monthly income for:				
	10 years	15 years	20 years	25 years	Indefinitely
6%	$ 90,000	$119,000	$140,000	$155,000	$200,000
7	86,000	111,000	129,000	141,000	171,000
8	82,000	105,000	120,000	130,000	150,000
9	79,000	99,000	111,000	119,000	133,000
10	76,000	93,000	104,000	110,000	120,000
12	70,000	83,000	91,000	95,000	100,000
15	62,000	71,000	76,000	78,000	80,000

*Compounded monthly.

profits decline, but they can go up when profits rise. Utilities are a good example of an industry group with a history of regular dividend increases.

As pointed out above, successful companies in other fields may also increase their dividends, and investors are likely to get substantial appreciation as well. In a pension plan, it makes no difference taxwise whether the return on your investment comes from income or growth. That's why many professional investment managers use "total return" as a yardstick to compare the merits of different types of securities.

Take a stock, XYZ, that gains 10 percent during a year and pays a dividend of 3 percent. Compare that investment with another, PQR, which gains only 6 percent but pays 7 percent. The total return on both is 13 percent, but XYZ is a better selection for a taxable portfolio because the larger capital-gain component means that the after-tax return will be higher than with PQR. The pension investor gets 13 percent with either, so he might base his preference on relative safety. Normally, a high-dividend stock like PQR figures to be less volatile than faster-growing XYZ, assuming that both companies are currently of good quality—and likely will continue to be.

This illustrates how stock selection can limit the risk in a pension plan while raising the expected return. Of course, the risk can be further reduced by maintaining a high ratio of bonds (and other fixed-income investments) to stocks (and other growth investments).

As far as practical, the degree of risk you willingly run in pension-plan investments should be governed by your estimate of your retirement needs and resources (See Box 7A). However, you also have to take the short-range economic outlook into account. Clearly, you'd want to lighten up on stocks if conditions turn bearish, and increase your stake in them when the market is bullish.

Stocks in your estate

The valuation and sale of stocks in publicly held corporations can easily be handled by the administrator of your estate. Nevertheless, stocks can sometimes pose vexing problems in an estate.

Dr. Jordan, for example, had a liking for highfliers. When he died, he left stocks worth $80,000, double what he'd paid. The executor, his eldest son, knew nothing about the stock market. He held on to the shares for several months, thinking he might need to sell them to pay estate expenses; when that proved unnecessary, he elected to distribute the stock to the heirs. By the time all the paperwork was completed, though, the market had plunged, and those volatile issues were down 40 percent in value.

To forestall recriminations, executors often sell out an estate's stock portfolio as soon as they're legally empowered to do so, especially if there's a shortage of other sources of cash. Yet that could prove disastrous. The market might be in a temporary downturn that it would be better to ride out. Or the sale might increase the heirs' income tax liability.

If you're getting on in years, you might consider weeding speculative issues out of your portfolio, perhaps replacing them with more stable blue chips or fixed-income investments. A large shareholder in a thinly capitalized company might be wise to lighten up gradually. Should you leave such a holding intact, your executor's dumping it could force the price down sharply. Shifting from a heavily margined account to a cash account now could also ease pressure on your executor later.

What should you do about stocks in which you have large paper profits? If you die owning them, your heirs won't have to pay a capital-gains tax on any appreciation that took place during your lifetime. However, the outlook for some of your investments or your present tax situation may prod you to realize profits while you live, without regard to the effect on your estate.

No matter what you do now, your executor will still have to make decisions about the stocks in your estate. If you think he'll need help, you can empower him in your will to hire investment counsel. Or you can appoint a knowledgeable co-executor. You might even put your executor in touch with your present financial adviser while you're still around.

Whoever manages your portfolio after you die should be free to act in response to market conditions. Your will shouldn't hamstring your executor with specific stock bequests or other restrictions. And as discussed below, your estate should contain enough liquid assets other than stocks so they won't have to be sold in untimely fashion to meet pressing cash needs.

BONDS AND OTHER FIXED-INCOME INVESTMENTS

A portfolio loaded with fast-growth stocks tends to exaggerate fluctuations of the market, swinging higher than the averages on the upside and lower on the downside. When a professional money manager has such a jittery portfolio under his wing and decides his client can't or shouldn't take the risks involved, he often turns to bonds for the balance and security the portfolio needs.

Bond prices are less volatile than stock prices. A bond's fixed payout to maturity tends to act as both floor and ceiling to limit changes in its resale value. And those changes are directed by shifts in the general interest rates, which normally take place gradually, although there are exceptions. As a bondholder, you're entitled to receive a specified amount of interest (the coupon rate) at regular intervals (usually twice a year) until the expiration date, when the bond's face value is paid to you.

Bond ratings are more reliable than stock ratings. Analysts can calculate a borrower company's debts, and its ability to earn at least enough to repay them in a specific number of years, with considerable precision. Original bond ratings sometimes have to be revised as the years go by, but no AAA bond (top quality) has defaulted since the Depression, and even at the BBB level (medium grade), experts can recall the failure of only Penn Central. Still, because a lower-rated bond is not quite as certain as a higher-rated one to pay interest and principal when due, it will sell for less even if the two are otherwise identical.

A $1,000 Carnation Company AAA bond, for example, carries an 8.5 percent interest coupon and matures in 1999. When it was selling at $810 for a yield to maturity (see Box 7B) of 11.0 percent, a Pfizer bond with the same coupon and maturity, but rated AA, was selling at $755 for a yield to maturity of 11.9 percent.

Bonds rated lower than AA will pay even higher interest, but the greater return isn't worth the considerably greater risk, unless your bond portfolio is well diversified and you're willing to continually monitor the financial fortunes of the corporations whose bonds you buy.

Many doctors favor bonds with long maturities when prevailing interest rates are relatively high, and go for shorter-term bonds when they're low. That way, they nail down good yields, and avoid locking themselves into poor ones. This approach is sensible, but it shouldn't be followed slavishly. For one thing, short bonds normally carry somewhat lower yields than long bonds of equal quality. Also, it's tricky to foretell the future direction of interest rates, as even experts admit.

By loading up on bonds with short maturities, you increase the investment decisions you have to make, and you could find yourself with a lot of

BOX 7B
Calculating bond yields

All bonds carry an interest rate pegged to their par value. Known as the "coupon rate," it's simply a specified percentage of the bond's face value. A $1,000 bond with a 6 percent coupon, for example, will pay interest of $60 annually.

But bond prices seldom stay at face value for long once trading in them begins. And when prices change, yields change. Let's assume the 6 percent bond is trading today at $920. The coupon still assures a $60 payout, so the current yield becomes 6.52 percent ($60 ÷ $920).

In comparing bonds, it's important to distinguish between "current yield" and "yield to maturity" (YTM). In the above case, when the bond matures, you'll receive $1,000—that is, $80 more than the $920 you paid. So your yield to maturity would be more than 6.52 percent. To figure the YTM requires some complicated calculations, but your broker can easily find it from a bond table. You'll want to know the YTM because it tells you whether a bond's quoted price is in line with those of others that may have different coupons and maturity dates.

If you should want to figure the YTM of a bond or note and there's no bond table handy, this worksheet gives a fair approximation. The example is for the 6 percent bond priced at $920, assuming a maturity date 10 years away:

	Sample figures	Your figures
A. Face value	$1,000	$ _____
B. Purchase price	920	_____
C. Discount (A − B)	80	_____
D. Years to maturity	10	_____
E. C ÷ D	8	_____
F. Coupon rate	6%	_____
G. Annual interest (A × F)	60	_____
H. E + G	68	_____
I. B + ½C	960	_____
J. Yield to maturity (100H ÷ I)	7.08%	_____

extra cash to place at a time when interest rates are down. If every year you're adding, say, $5,000 or $10,000 worth of bonds to your portfolio, you might do better to lean toward longer maturities and rely on the law of averages, instead of trying to anticipate the direction of interest rates.

If you feel that bonds have a place in your financial picture, but you'd rather not take on the job of assembling and supervising a bond portfolio yourself, an alternative is to invest in the shares of a mutual fund specializing in bonds. Because they can buy in large lots, diversify their commitments, and assess the risks more accurately than a nonprofessional, bond funds may produce a higher yield than you could prudently aim for if you managed your own bond portfolio. Also, you can reinvest income without waiting for it to accumulate. And the shares offer instant liquidity at publicly quoted prices. So you can save time and retain flexibility, with your money in expert hands.

Keep in mind, though, that bond-fund shares fluctuate in value, so you might incur a capital loss when you redeem them. Bonds you buy outright may also decline in value, but you have the option of selecting the more profitable ones for sale, if you need cash, and holding the others to maturity. There's also the possibility that a fund manager will take higher risks than you would in an effort to boost yields.

Bonds in your retirement plan

Bonds of financially strong, profitable corporations are prudent investments for a pension portfolio. They provide guaranteed, steady income for years to come, as well as preservation of principal, so that you can be confident of meeting future obligations to plan participants. However, there are a few pitfalls to guard against.

Although you're virtually certain to get your original investment back when you hold a high-quality bond to maturity, you may incur a loss if you have to sell it sooner, because bond values fluctuate with changing interest rates. In a tax-sheltered plan, the loss is especially vexing since it confers no tax benefit.

To avoid possible forced sales under unfavorable market conditions, you might want to select bonds that mature at times when plan participants are expected to retire. Since retirement dates may vary and some vested employees may leave prematurely, staggered maturities may be best. A third of your bonds could be long-term, perhaps 15 years or more; another third medium-term, eight to 15 years of so; and the rest short-term. Such a mix should give you a satisfactory average yield, yet offer protection against market hazards.

If you opt for long or even intermediate maturities, you may also need protection against premature redemption by the bond issuer. If a bond has a high coupon rate, the issuer may "call" it (pay it off) when rates decline, then borrow for less. Ordinarily the call price is higher than face value, so you get some profit unless you bought the bond at a price above call. But the gain probably won't compensate for the fact that you'll now be forced to reinvest the bond proceeds at a lower yield than you'd figured on originally.

To avoid that, you can choose corporate bonds that aren't callable, but they're a rare species. More common are bonds with a deferred-call clause. This means they can't be called for a specified period after issue—usually five to 10 years. Of course, you'll pay for such protection in the form of somewhat lower yield than is available on similar bonds without it.

Another way to deal with the premature-redemption problem is to buy bonds that were issued when interest rates were substantially below current levels. They carry relatively low coupons and are accordingly priced at a discount from face value. Low-coupon bonds aren't likely to be called because the issuers can't borrow more cheaply.

Low-coupon bonds may have another advantage besides providing call protection. Suppose you have $10,000 to invest in one of two 15-year bonds of equal quality. Both of the bonds offer you the same yield to maturity—9 percent. However, bond A has a 9 percent coupon and sells at face value, while bond B has a 4 percent coupon and therefore sells at a discount. Which is the better investment for your retirement plan?

You'd get the same total return if you hold either bond to maturity and if you reinvest each coupon payment at 9 percent compounded. That second "if" is the big one. Remember, bond interest doesn't compound automatically like savings-account interest. It's paid to you twice yearly, and you have to invest it somewhere else. There's no guarantee that you can achieve an average reinvestment rate as high as 9 percent over 15 years.

What if your average reinvestment rate turns out to be only 7 percent? Then the low-coupon bond would net you around $1,000 more in total return than the high-coupon bond. With a 6 percent average reinvestment rate, the figure would be $1,500. These calculations ignore taxes since they're irrelevant in a retirement-plan portfolio. And they assume that the high-coupon bond won't be called; if it were, you'd be even worse off.

Be sure that you distinguish between good-quality bonds, selling at discounts because their coupons are low, and so-called junk bonds, whose bargain prices are due to poor ratings. Though junk bonds often carry outsize yields, their risk is excessive for most retirement plans.

In addition to bonds, a portion of your pension assets might go into certificates of deposit, Treasury bills and notes, and money-market funds. By staggering the maturities of the CDs and Treasuries, from perhaps six months to four years, you'll get a reasonable average yield without locking yourself in for too long. The amount you keep in such holdings should depend on market trends. If interest rates seem headed downwards, a switch to longer-term bonds or even to stocks may be in order. If rates are on the rise and conditions turn bearish, temporize by increasing your short-term income investments.

The prescription for a retirement portfolio is to diversify enough to produce a good average yield over the plan's lifetime with a minimum of risk. A reasonable yield to aim for is two or three percentage points above the current rate of inflation.

One of the simplest ways to raise your return is to make your retirement-plan contributions early in the year. If you contribute $20,000 to your plan at the end of every year and earn 10 percent on the money, you'll have about $319,000 in 10 years. But if you make the same contribution at the beginning of each year and earn the same 10 percent, your fund will grow to more than

$350,000. To accumulate that much via year-end contributions, you'd need to earn 12 percent.

Fixed-income investments for estate liquidity

In the months after your death, your family and executor will need cash for living costs, the funeral, and other final expenses. Very likely, the money you keep in bank accounts, Treasury bills, and other short-term investments will be ample to pay those expenses. But the legal formalities involved in transferring ownership of short-term investments may take a month or more. Even joint bank accounts with your spouse may be frozen temporarily—though usually only for a matter of days or weeks. Bank time deposits and savings certificates may be subject to penalties for premature withdrawal, though most banks will waive them in the event of death. (Waiver is automatic in the case of Keogh accounts.)

Insurance can help provide cash for debts, administrative expenses, taxes, and specific bequests you may have made in your will. But you should also consider putting a portion of your capital into fixed-income investments that can either benefit your heirs if you die prematurely or help support you when you retire.

The main drawback of fixed-income investments outside your pension plan is that the interest they pay adds to your tax load while you're alive. One way to minimize that burden—while still locking in current high yields—is to buy discount bonds issued before June 28, 1984. You're taxed only on their low current interest until they mature. Then your profit—the difference between their face value and your discounted purchase price—will be taxed as a capital gain.

Bonds issued by states, cities, or local government agencies—known collectively as ''municipals''—avoid federal income tax altogether. In return for the tax exemption, you'll have to accept a yield that's below what you may be able to get from other investments. You can increase your after-tax yield by choosing municipals issued in your state, since they are normally exempt from state and local as well as federal income taxes (see Box 7C).

This tax break, however, won't be much help to your heirs if they're in a low tax bracket. So they may want to sell the municipals to pay expenses or invest elsewhere at higher yields. What they get for the bonds will be their market price then, not their face value. Bear in mind that the closer a bond is to maturity, the closer its price is to the face value. Thus, if you're choosing bonds for estate liquidity rather than long-term income, select issues with relatively short maturities—five years or so—and replace them with similar bonds as they mature.

Federal government bonds may also have a place in your plan. They're safer and more readily marketable than municipal or corporate issues. Their yield may be a few percentage points above that of municipals and is usually exempt from state and local income taxes, though subject to federal tax.

BOX 7C
Tax-exempt yield worksheet

The higher your federal income tax bracket, the more valuable a tax-exempt return is. You'll do even better if the yield is also exempt from state and city income taxes, as it may be if you own a bond issued by a municipality in your state. To see how much you'd benefit, start by figuring your combined top tax bracket. (This calculation allows for the fact that state and city taxes are deductible from your federal tax; if you don't itemize deductions on your federal return, use the sum of lines A and C on line E.) The next two steps let you calculate your yield multiplier. Apply this figure (line G) to the nominal yield of any tax-exempt bond to see how much a taxable investment would have to yield for the same return.

	Sample figures	Your figures
A. Top federal tax bracket	45.0%	_____
B. Subtract line A from 100	55.0%	_____
C. Top local tax bracket (state + city)	10.0%	_____
D. Multiply B by C and divide by 100	5.5%	_____
E. Combined top tax bracket (A + D)	50.5%	_____
F. Subtract E from 100	49.5%	_____
G. Your yield multiplier (100 ÷ F)	2.02	_____
H. Nominal yield of tax-exempt bond	9.0%	_____
I. Equivalent taxable yield (G × H)	18.2%	_____

Even the federal income tax can be minimized if you own Series EE Savings Bonds. Yields on these US bonds are tied to—but somewhat lower than—money market rates. Holders have the option of deferring tax payment on them until they cash them in. Eventually the tax must be paid, but it needn't amount to much if your heirs are in a low bracket or if they redeem the bonds over a period of years.

REAL ESTATE INVESTMENTS

Investing in real estate calls for a high degree of expertise, for capital that can be tied up over extended periods, and for a willingness to take risks that are sometimes substantial. If the description fits you, then real estate may offer you an effective tax shelter, a reassuring hedge against inflation, and a source of potentially large capital gains.

Depreciation and the leverage provided by borrowed money are two of the keys to real estate profits. A doctor who acquires a $250,000 building with a down payment of $50,000 and a $200,000 mortgage can claim depreciation deductions on $250,000—five times his cash outlay. If he later sells the building for $300,000, he's doubled his money, even though the value has gone up only 20 percent. Of course, if the building's value *declines* 20 percent to $200,000, all of the $50,000 investment is down the drain. Because leverage is two-edged, you must use it with prudence.

Real estate in your retirement plan

Some plan advisers turn thumbs down on real estate, even though they concede it can be an excellent source of income and a counterweight to long-term inflation. For one thing, depreciation deductions and other tax benefits are of little or no use in a tax-sheltered pension plan. For another, real property is a lot harder to sell than securities in case a plan suddenly needs cash. This lack of liquidity can be particularly troublesome for a multidoctor practice if it breaks up and plan assets have to be distributed.

Even if you don't want to take on the problems of property ownership in your plan, it can still benefit from real estate appreciation by becoming a lender. When credit is short and interest rates are high, borrowers may be willing to give lenders a share of their property's future appreciation in return for a mortgage loan below bank interest rates.

Another way to put real estate into your retirement portfolio is via so-called commingled funds (akin to mutual funds) sponsored by banks, insurance companies, brokerage firms, and other financial institutions. They make it about as easy for pension plans—corporate, Keogh, and IRA—to invest in real estate as in stocks or bonds.

Many commingled funds invest in commercial or industrial properties, but some go in for apartment complexes, while others stick to equity-appreciation mortgages. Thus, you can choose a fund whose investment approach is consistent with your retirement plan's requirements for safety and liquidity as well as for growth and income.

A number of commingled funds catering to pension plans haven't been around long enough to be judged on their past performance. Some sponsors, though, have run nonpension real estate funds for years or have engaged in other realty ventures. Ask to see the sponsor's track record on those operations. And find out how experienced the sponsor is in acquiring and managing real estate, as well as in financing it. If the prospectus isn't sufficiently revealing, don't hesitate to ask the sponsor for answers before you commit yourself and your retirement fund.

In contrast to stock mutual funds, real estate funds can't liquidate their assets quickly to raise money for redemptions, so they have to rely mainly on their cash reserves. Those are usually sufficient to handle redemptions as long as cash continues to flow in from sales of new shares. But if a fund's investors ever make a concerted rush for the exit, redemption could be slowed or suspended. What's more, if you redeem in a bear market, you'll get reduced value for your holding. (Some funds aren't obligated to redeem your shares, though the sponsor may help you locate a prospective purchaser for them.)

Sponsors of commingled funds recommend—and sometimes require—that pension plans invest only a fraction of their total capital in fund shares. The suggested limits range from 5 to 20 percent, but you should let your particular circumstances decide. Doctors who are certain they won't be under pressure to cash in real estate investments for, say, 10 years or longer might not want to be bound by an arbitrary limit. However, you should still aim for flexibility and greater safety by using more than one commingled fund or by putting some money into other real estate investments.

Realty in your estate

Investment real estate may be a good way to build your fortune, but it could become an albatross around the necks of your heirs. Take Dr. Allen, for instance. He believes in the old saying: "God isn't making any more land, but he's still making people." Accordingly, Allen put $100,000 of his capital into a choice parcel of raw land. Recently, he refused an offer of $300,000 for the property. Although he has to pay growing taxes on the land, his ample practice income allows him to bear the expense without strain while he waits for even better offers.

Should he die, however, his practice income will stop, and his widow could find herself in a jam if most of his liquid assets had to go for estate taxes and expenses. What's left might not yield enough income to meet rising real estate taxes and support the family as well. Forced into a quick sale, Mrs. Allen might have to take a beating on the land.

One solution would be for Dr. Allen to sell some of the property now and put the proceeds into more liquid investments, such as stocks and bonds. Another possibility would be to lease part or all of the land to a developer, so that it would *produce* income instead of drain it.

Unlike Dr. Allen, Dr. Belden has made his real estate investments in income-producing property. He owns two garden-apartment developments in his town that yield a steady stream of cash. Despite his busy practice, Belden keeps close tabs on their operations and handles most of the management chores himself. He does a good job of it because he's well organized and has a talent for business.

Unfortunately, the family members who'll inherit the buildings aren't similarly endowed. In their hands, the property is likely to go downhill and eventually be sold for far less than it ought to bring. To prevent that, Dr. Belden could sell the property now, but then he'd have to pay a large capital-gains tax. Instead, he should weigh other options:

One is to swap the apartment buildings for a different kind of real estate that would give his heirs fewer headaches. If the deal involved no cash payment to Belden, the swap wouldn't result in a taxable capital gain.

A second alternative would be to sell a part interest to a trustworthy associate or relative capable of shouldering management responsibility. That way Belden's family would still be assured of receiving some income from the property. And Belden could minimize his capital-gains tax liability by taking payment in installments rather than all at once.

If neither of these solutions proves practicable, Belden should look around for a suitable professional manager. He could leave the job of hiring one to his heirs after his death, but he's under less pressure than they would be and in a much better position to check on the man's performance. True, the management fees will reduce income from the property, but Belden's family stands to come out ahead in the long run.

Dr. Carvon is a different case. She doesn't need or want income. She's investing in real estate primarily for tax savings. For instance, she put $100,000 into a partnership in a shopping center that's yielding her only $3,000 a year. But it also gives her $20,000 in annual depreciation deductions. That boosts her after-tax return on the investment to more than 10 percent. When she dies, though, those depreciation deductions will do her heirs little good because of their relatively low tax brackets.

This doesn't mean Dr. Carvon must give up what, for her, is a lucrative investment. She should simply recognize that her heirs may have to liquidate it in order to invest for a higher yield. In doing that, they may take a loss. If Carvon has too many tax-shelter investments, her family could end up with a much smaller inheritance than she anticipates. So she should diversify sufficiently to guard against this possibility.

Aside from economic difficulties, real estate holdings can sometimes cause your heirs and executor tax and administrative problems, unless forethought is taken. Suppose you leave property to someone other than your spouse, involving a sizable estate tax. Do you want that person to pay it, or should it come out of your spouse's or some other heirs' shares? As pointed out in Chapter 2, the wrong party may get stuck with the tax burden if your will doesn't spell out your wishes.

If the property is mortgaged, your will should specify whether the liability is to remain with the property. In many states, a mortgage is considered a debt that must be paid by the estate, unless you indicate otherwise.

Do you own a working farm? Such property may be worth less as a farm than if put to some other use—a housing development, for example. If the family member inheriting it intends to operate the farm, your executor may choose the lower valuation for estate tax purposes. But this will increase your heir's taxable capital gain if he later sells the property; and he may also have to give back part or all of the estate-tax saving if the sale takes place (or family farming ceases) within 10 years of your death. So you'd do well to talk things over with the prospective heir and instruct your executor accordingly.

Whatever investment real estate you have, bear in mind that prices respond sharply to fluctuating interest rates and economic ups and downs. Since you can't know what market conditions will be like when you die, the more leeway you can give your executor, the better. If feasible, let him consult with your heirs and distribute the various properties as they wish, selling off those no one wants, in due course, and dividing the proceeds equitably. Where appropriate your will should authorize the executor to lease out properties while waiting for a favorable opportunity to sell them.

In some states, the law automatically gives an executor broad powers to act in the heirs' best interests. But to be safe, your will should grant them to the executor specifically as your holdings require.

For the utmost flexibility, consider placing your properties in a trust that allows you to control them until you die, then lets the trustee manage and dispose of them as you've directed. This arrangement is particularly desirable when you own real property in several states. Otherwise, there would probably have to be probate proceedings in each state.

As pointed out in Chapter 4, such a living trust can be used to consolidate all your assets and greatly facilitate the handling and transfer of your estate. Moreover, the trustee can take the current management of your investments off your shoulders, if you want to be free of the responsibility or are worried what would happen to them in case you fell ill.

If all you want to do is avoid multiple probate, you can simply give away ownership of your out-of-state property. Suppose you have a vacation retreat that the whole family uses, and no one cares who holds title to it. Putting it in someone else's name while you're alive can save trouble and administrative expense later on, though it won't dodge gift or estate tax. Or consider transferring the property to a corporation. That eliminates probate and possibly estate tax as well, if you give the stock away piecemeal.

8

Benefits your corporation can provide

Your professional corporation is a business entity that has a legal existence separate from you and other shareholders. It employs you, your colleagues, and your staff; collects practice income and pays expenses, including salaries and pension and insurance benefits; and acquires and disposes of corporate assets. All this yields tax and other advantages, some of which have estate-planning implications. Look at the corporate gains you may make from retirement plans, insurance benefits, retained earnings, ancillary corporations, and trust leasebacks.

CORPORATE RETIREMENT PLANS

An incorporated doctor's pension contribution can be greater than an unincorporated doctor's, even when they have identical pension plans and the same amount of practice revenue and expense. Here's how:

Expenses for a professional car, travel to meetings and conventions, practice-building entertainment, continuing education, journals and books, and professional licensing and association fees can be paid either by the corporation and deducted on its income tax return, or by the doctor-employee and deducted as unreimbursed business expenses on his personal return. If your corporation adopts the latter policy, it can increase your total compensation accordingly, since it won't be paying those expenses directly. The effect is to increase the base for your retirement-plan contributions.

Suppose your corporation currently puts the maximum 25 percent of your salary into a defined-contribution plan. Then for every dollar of expenses shifted from the corporation to yourself, another 20 cents can go into the plan. Say those corporation-paid expenses are $10,000 and your total compensation is now $70,000 (salary $56,000 and maximum plan contribution $14,000). If the $10,000 is shifted to you, your compensation becomes $80,000 (salary $64,000 and maximum plan contribution $16,000). Deducting the $10,000 from salary leaves you $54,000. Thus, you've reduced your taxable income by $2,000 and increased your retirement-plan stake by the same amount.

You needn't shift all your expenses, of course. Your employment contract can specify which you'll pay and which the corporation will pay. Make sure that you adhere to the contract precisely. If you're ever audited and the IRS finds that you've paid an expense the corporation was obligated to pay, the agent may disallow the deduction on your personal return. And it will be too late to go back and claim the expense on behalf of the corporation.

Borrowing plan funds

This option is available only to doctors with corporate plans, *not to those with Keogh plans.* The law lays down a set of loan rules that shouldn't prove too hard to follow for most doctors. Generally, your loans outstanding can total no more than half your vested amount in the plan. You can borrow more than half if your total loan balance is $10,000 or less, but in no case can the total be more than $50,000.

You must repay the loan in five years. There is one exception: You can take longer if you use the money for a principal residence (not a vacation home) for yourself or a family member. Whatever the loan's purpose, you must pay a reasonable rate of interest, furnish adequate security, and set up a schedule to repay the loan.

The loan privilege allows you to get the full benefit of tax-deductible plan contributions, yet still retain limited access to the funds for personal purposes. (The corporation itself, however, is prohibited from borrowing from the pension fund.) If your present plan doesn't offer loan privileges, it can be amended to do so.

Keep in mind that if you make it easy for yourself to borrow, it will also be easy for your vested employees, because the plan must not discriminate. So you might do well to adopt tougher restrictions on borrowing than the law requires. That would help protect your employees—and yourself—against borrowing frivolously and being unable to repay on schedule.

What happens if you don't repay all the money within five years? The amount still outstanding at the end of the period will be treated as a premature distribution, subject to a 10 percent penalty tax. Also, it's added to your income, so you're actually taxed twice.

If you leave before retirement

If you're in a multidoctor corporation and depart before you reach retirement age, what happens to your pension money? Even though you gave up part of your income to fund the plan, you could lose some of that money if you're not fully vested.

To protect you and the other doctors, the plan might provide that a departing employee can carry his entire retirement fund from one corporation to another. By allowing portability, you may be able to transfer the vested and unvested assets from your present corporation to a new one you join or start.

If you're leaving private practice or aren't joining a new corporation, you can't take the unvested portion with you. However, you can switch the vested portion to an IRA. If you later join another corporation, you can then switch the money from the IRA to your new corporate plan.

Alternatively, a clause in your employment contract could guarantee you severance pay to compensate for the amount of pension money you leave behind. Of course, if you become disabled or die, the plan should provide that you or your beneficiary gets the entire fund.

INSURANCE BENEFITS

A professional corporation can tax-deduct premiums for group term life insurance, though the insured individual must pay tax on premiums for coverage above $50,000. While the corporation needn't provide a uniform amount of protection for all employees, it must give all full-timers some coverage if there are fewer than 10 of them on the payroll.

The precise amount of insurance coverage for each of the employees in your practice can be based on a percentage of their salaries. Thus, if the corporation provided coverage equal to 50 percent of the first $100,000 of salary, doctors earning that much or more would get the maximum tax-free amount. Other employees would also be insured for 50 percent of their salaries, but the dollar amount would be much less, so the premiums you'd have to pay would be correspondingly smaller. Moreover, premiums for women should be lower than for men the same age. Still, it's going to cost you something to insure your entire staff. So when considering a group plan, compare its after-tax cost with the amount you'd have to pay for the coverage you'd have to go out and get on your own.

If the basic cost of group life insurance isn't prohibitive, you may want more than $50,000. Though you'll personally have to pay tax on some of the premium for coverage in excess of $50,000, you'll still get a break. For example, a doctor under 40 who has $100,000 of group term life—twice the nontaxable limit—would be taxed on less than $70 of the annual premium the corpo-

BOX 8A
Tax on group term life insurance

If you receive more than $50,000 of such coverage from your corporation, the cost of the excess is taxable income to you, but the taxable amount is based on rates set by the IRS, not on what the corporation actually paid. For example, a 57-year-old doctor with $150,000 of group term life insurance would have to pay tax on $900 income (10 times the amount shown in the table). The IRS revises these rates periodically.

Age	Annual rate per $10,000 of insurance
30-34	$ 10.80
35-39	13.20
40-44	20.40
45-49	34.80
50-54	57.60
55-59	90.00
60 or older	140.40

ration paid for him. The tax liability increases with age (see Box 8A), as does the premium.

You'll have more flexibility if your group plan provides for separate contracts instead of one master policy. The individual contracts will allow you to continue term coverage if you ever leave the corporation. If you're covered by a master contract, you must convert the insurance to a whole life policy when you leave.

Special-purpose life insurance

In addition to tax-deductible group term or retirement-plan coverage (see Chapter 6), your corporation can take out insurance on your life, with itself as beneficiary, to pay certain expenses that would arise at your death. While the costs of this insurance can't be written off for tax purposes, it's paid out of the corporation's lightly taxed income, so it might take less than $1.20 of pretax earnings to pay $1.00 of premium. If you paid it yourself, that might take as much as $2.00 of your personal pretax income.

Here's an example of a contingency the insurance could cover: Suppose you have a severance-pay arrangement whereby the corporation will pay you a specified sum each year after you leave, and if you die while still employed, the money will be paid to your family. That's where the insurance comes in. Let's say the corporation agreed to pay $10,000 a year for 10 years. With an insurance policy for an appropriate amount, the corporation could pay the money without strain. (The proceeds of the insurance would be tax-free to the corporation.) If you live until retirement, the corporation can use the policy's accumulated cash value to fund your annual severance payments.

Another special purpose for insurance: to provide funds to fulfill a stock-redemption agreement. The corporation insures the life of each doctor shareholder for an amount equal to the value of his stock. When a shareholder dies, the corporation collects on the policy and pays for the stock. Although the corporation can't tax-deduct the payment, it isn't taxed on the insurance proceeds. That way, everybody benefits. The deceased doctor's family gets the money for his shares right away, and the remaining shareholders don't have to come up with large sums of cash, nor are they currently taxed on the increased value of their stock.

A policy payable to the corporation could also be used to finance a $5,000 death benefit to your spouse or family. That much is free of estate and income tax. The policy proceeds go to the corporation tax-free, and it can take a deduction for the $5,000 payment.

Before buying such insurance, check with your tax adviser. If there are fewer than five shareholders in the corporation, it could be hit with a special tax if the corporate profits are used for insurance. Also, there may be adverse estate tax consequences.

Postretirement life insurance

In recent years, insurance companies have been offering professional corporations a way to extend coverage beyond retirement and thereby increase tax-deductible fringe benefits. The corporation builds up the insurance fund—called Retired Lives Reserves—with tax-deductible contributions during your working years.

Some advisers object to the arrangement because the funds are tied to the insurance company sponsoring the plan. You can avoid that drawback by setting up a fund within your corporation. This kind of arrangement will increase administrative costs because the corporation will have to hire an actuary to compute the contributions and to keep track of the assets. However, it will give you complete freedom to manage the assets and to take the money instead of the insurance coverage when you retire.

Disability coverage

An unincorporated doctor can't tax-deduct the premiums he pays for disability insurance, but any benefits he collects are tax-free. If a professional corporation pays the premiums, the benefits are taxable, but the premiums are deductible by the corporation. So the doctor-shareholder in effect pays for his insurance with pretax dollars.

You'll nearly always do better to opt for deductible premiums (through the corporation) when you're healthy and in a high tax bracket, even if you later have to pay taxes on the benefits.

Not all your disability benefits come from insurance coverage. You'll also get payments from your corporation if you're disabled. In a solo corporation, you'll simply continue to draw your salary as long as there's money to pay it. It's more complex in a multidoctor corporation. Employment contracts should deal with the following questions to avoid trouble later: Should the corporation cover partial disability? How should the corporation handle recurrent disability? When should a sick doctor be forced to retire?

If you join a multidoctor corporation, check on the way the monthly disability benefit in your contract is figured. It may be based on a percentage of your salary, not including bonuses. If your corporation elects to pay big bonuses, that could make an important difference. Also, be sure to check whether any of your policies deduct corporate benefits from the benefits they pay. Again, that could make a major difference in the amount of disability income you would receive.

The accounts receivable that you may have generated before becoming disabled go to the corporation. So it's equitable for a multidoctor corporation to carry a disabled MD for some months, usually on a declining percentage basis. This would be a typical arrangement: 100 percent of salary for the first three or four months, tapering down to 75 percent, 50 percent, and 25 percent in segments of a few months each.

Corporate groups also frequently provide severance pay for doctors who have to leave because of disability. Generally, the best way to fund such benefits is through disability insurance with long waiting periods, but a large group can usually manage to fund the severance benefit without insurance. The employment contract should be worded so that the money the departing physician receives for his share of the corporation's assets (furniture, fixtures, equipment, and building) is treated as a return of capital and is therefore tax-free to him. The part of the severance pay that represents accounts receivable will be taxed as ordinary income and should be spread over more than one year if practicable.

RETAINED EARNINGS

If you take all your corporate earnings (after expenses and retirement-plan contributions) as salary and bonuses, the corporation pays no income tax. But you, of course, are taxed on all the income—in some cases as high as 50 percent. However, annual earnings retained by the corporation are taxed at only 15 percent on the first $25,000; 18 percent on the next $25,000; and 30 percent on the next $25,000.

If you don't need all the earnings for living expenses, you'd have more after-tax dollars to invest by leaving some of the money in the corporation. Not only that, but 85 percent of the corporation's income from dividends on its investments in stocks of other corporations is tax-exempt. For example, a corporation with $60,000 in preferred stocks paying 10 percent dividends would get $6,000 a year but pay tax on just $900. That would cost only $135 if the corporation is in the 15 percent bracket. Note, however, that if your professional corporation sells stock at a loss, it can't write that off against practice income, but only against investment gains.

If a professional corporation's retained earnings over the years reach $150,000, any additional amount retained is hit by a heavy penalty tax on top of the regular corporate income tax. The penalty can be avoided if some of the surplus is set aside for a specific corporate purpose—say, to buy a medical building or equipment for the corporation.

When a doctor-stockholder leaves the corporation, or if it's liquidated, his share of the surplus is taxable to him as a long-term capital gain. Although, in effect, retained earnings are taxed twice—first in the year earned, then on retirement or liquidation—the total tax may well be no more than 32 percent. Thus, a solo corporation retaining $10,000 of its earnings in a given year would pay $1,500 in corporate income tax, leaving $8,500. When the doctor eventually gets the money, he'll pay a maximum capital-gains tax of $1,700 (20 percent of $8,500), leaving him $6,800.

ANCILLARY CORPORATIONS

Chapter 10 describes the tax benefits of sharing ownership of assets with low-bracket family members. You can't give them stock in your professional corporation, but they can share in the assets and income of a separate corporation that offers practice-related services. For instance, you could incorporate a laboratory or dispensary and turn your stock over to a custodian for your children.

To pass muster with the IRS, the ancillary corporation must not perform "substantially all" of its services for your professional corporation. So the ancillary corporation should either deal with (and charge) patients directly, or it should perform services for other medical practices, as in the case of a cardiologist whose lab develops heart monitor printouts for several practices.

To avoid being accused of retaining control of the stock, you do well to name someone other than yourself or your spouse as custodian. Be sure, too, that you segregate the corporation's funds, make timely distribution of profits, and otherwise deal with it at arm's length. It's safer not to borrow from the corporation, though that's not prohibited if done properly.

Income can be passed to stockholders (and taxed in their low brackets) without paying corporate tax if the corporation is set up under Subchapter S of the Internal Revenue Code. But if you don't draw a reasonable salary from

Estate planning strategies for physicians

BOX 8B
Bequests of controlling stock interests

Do you expect to leave your heirs a controlling stock interest in a nonmedical corporation? If so, be on the lookout for both a tax trap and a tax break.

The tax trap: Your heirs may want to get cash out of the corporation by having it redeem part of the stock, while holding on to enough to keep control. In that case, the money will be taxable to them as ordinary income.* The law treats such partial redemptions as dividends, not as proceeds from the sale of capital assets. Your heirs can get capital-gains tax treatment by selling shares outside the corporation, or by having it redeem substantially all their stock, giving up control; then there might be no income tax at all, since the heirs' cost basis for the stock is its value at your death. But neither of those alternatives may prove to be feasible or desirable for your heirs.

The tax break: Your heirs can make a partial redemption and still get capital-gains treatment if (1) the amount they receive isn't more than the total of death taxes and estate administration expenses they owe, and (2) the value of all the shares you leave exceeds 35 percent of your estate.

Suppose your estate (after subtracting debts and administrative expenses) figures to be about $1 million, and you estimate that the corporation stock is worth $320,000. By giving away some $100,000 of other assets (to your spouse, for instance), you could reduce your future estate to $900,000; then your stock holding would meet the 35 percent requirement. Putting more of your money into the corporation now to push the value of your stock above $350,000 would achieve the same result.

Note: Proceeds from partial stock redemptions you make while alive (including professional-corporation shares) will also be taxed as ordinary income if you retain corporate control. The IRS rationale is that the decrease in the number of your shares hasn't changed your investment position meaningfully; you're merely taking some of the corporation's earnings or surplus as a disguised dividend. In this context, you may be considered as retaining control if stock is held by members of your family or other businesses you own.

---

* The value of the stock is also subject to estate tax, which may be deductible for income tax purposes.

---

work for a Sub-S corporation, the IRS can allocate part of the profits as compensation to you. That wouldn't happen with a regular corporation, but then you have the double-tax problem to consider. Your accountant can help you choose the right type of corporation. You'll also need guidance if you intend to leave your heirs a controlling stock interest in a corporation (see Box 8B).

Setting up a family business as a partnership rather than a corporation may also yield tax benefits (see Box 10E).

TRUST-LEASEBACKS

Such arrangements may allow incorporated doctors to shift income to lower-bracket recipients by giving them ownership of practice assets. One New York ophthalmologist put his office furniture and equipment into a temporary trust for his three children. Then his professional corporation leased the assets from the trust for an annual fee averaging about $9,000. Thus, the corporation's rent became a tax-deductible business expense, and the money became the children's income. By carrying out this trust-leaseback procedure, the doctor deflected the rental payments from his high tax bracket into his children's lower ones.

Over the years, the tax savings helped to finance the children's college educations and get them started in their careers. When the trust ended after more than 10 years, the assets were returned to the corporation. Unfortunately, the doctor had to battle the IRS in court to preserve his tax benefits—but he won out.

In recent years, precedents have been building up in favor of trust-leasebacks. In addition to the Tax Court, most of the US circuit courts of appeals where the issue has come up have ruled for the taxpayers—the majority of them doctors. Many of the decisions have identified four elements that tip the balance in their favor:

☐ *An independent trustee.* Taxpayers have fared best when they've appointed a bank to administer the trust without any written restrictions. Some courts, however, have ruled favorably when the trustee was an attorney or even a close relative. You're asking for trouble if you name yourself trustee.

☐ *A written lease and realistic rent payments.* Even with an independent trustee, taxpayers have had a rough time with the IRS when they were unable to produce a written lease. What's more, the rent paid the trust must be in line with what commercial lessors in the area charge. These elements not only are important in themselves, but also may help you clear the next hurdle.

☐ *A bona fide business purpose.* While some judges have ruled against trust-leasebacks on grounds that they're really shams, most taxpayers have been able to convince the courts that there is, indeed, substance to arrangements of this sort.

☐ *A complete transfer of the assets.* If the courts feel that either the trust or the trustee is under the taxpayer's control, they will hold that he hasn't given up his dominion over the assets. The best way to avoid this problem is to set up the trust so that the assets are transferred to your spouse or children when the trust terminates.

The more of those elements present in the arrangement, the safer you are. Thus, the safest trust-leaseback is one in which assets are given away without any expectation of getting them back, and a completely independent trustee negotiates a lease at a reasonable rental.

What happens when the trust terminates and the assets go to the children, who by then are presumably adults? After so many years, the equipment's actual value should be minimal. The corporation or the individual doctor could therefore buy the assets back for a nominal amount. Or if it's still desirable to transfer income to the children, the lease can be extended—and without a trustee as middleman, now that the children are of age.

Equipment may be transferred to the trust by gift or sale. How the transfer should be made depends on who originally owns the assets. If the professional corporation owns the equipment, it should be formally sold to the trust; the trust can pay for it in installments, out of future lease income. If the equipment is in the doctor's name, it can be given to the trust. Either way, it should be independently appraised.

9

Preserve your practice's value for your estate

If you're in a partnership or multidoctor corporation, you'll want to make certain that your heirs receive the full value of your share of the practice assets in case you die in harness. Of course, the doctor or doctors associated with you will want the same assurance for their own heirs. To achieve this mutual objective, you and your associates should decide beforehand how such a contingency is to be dealt with.

BUY-SELL AGREEMENT

The usual procedure is to draw up an agreement specifying that a departing associate, or his estate if deceased, must sell his interest to the remaining doctors, and that they, in turn, must buy it. How the agreement is legally structured depends on whether the association practice is incorporated. In any event, the agreement should:

☐ Contain a formula for determining the value of an associate's share at his death or separation from the practice for disability or other reasons.

☐ Specify the time and manner of payment—whether in a lump sum or in installments with interest.

☐ Guarantee the availability of cash for the payout—usually by providing that insurance is to be carried on the life of each member of the practice. If separation is other than by death, the insurance can be cashed in or other provision made to fund the payout.

In a partnership, the survivors, as the insurance beneficiaries, use the proceeds to purchase the departed partner's interest. Such a "cross-purchase" arrangement can also be used when the practice is incorporated, but there's an alternative: Instead of the survivors buying the stock personally, the corporation itself can redeem the stock. Either way, if you sell out while still alive, there may be a taxable capital gain. If your estate sells the shares, there normally wouldn't be, since its cost basis for the shares is their value at the time of your death. Of course, the stock's value is subject to estate tax.

Whichever method your buy-sell agreement calls for, the premiums on the insurance to fund it are not tax-deductible expenses. That usually makes it cheaper for the corporation to buy the insurance, since its tax bracket is almost certainly lower than the individual doctors'. It's also simpler for the corporation to do it when there are more than two or three doctors involved.

If you're now in a multidoctor practice, you may already be covered by such an agreement. But if it was drawn up some time ago, its provisions may be outmoded by changes in the tax laws or in your financial or family circumstances. A thorough review of the agreement by an estate-planning specialist might pay dividends for you and your associates.

You may belong to a medical group that has set up a separate corporation or partnership to own practice-related assets, such as equipment or real estate. If a separate buy-sell agreement is involved, that one deserves careful scrutiny, too.

One doctor should have had the agreement reviewed when he and a group of colleagues formed a corporation to own and operate a medical supply business. They agreed that the corporation should carry insurance on each shareholder, ostensibly to buy back the stock if one should die. But the agreement didn't specify that the insurance *must* be used that way. When the doctor died, the other stockholders used the proceeds to reduce the corporation's outstanding debt. That left his widow with the stock instead of cash. Although the stock's value had increased because the debt was lowered, it was even harder to sell for its fair price. (For tax aspects of nonmedical corporation stock redemption, see Box 8B.)

CHOICES FOR A SOLO PRACTITIONER

While you're alive, your practice may be the most valuable asset you have. But even if it's an exceptionally lucrative one, its value is apt to dissipate rapidly after your death if you're a solo practitioner. Patients drift off, and soon the practice vanishes. At a forced sale, equipment and patients' records may bring only a fraction of what they were worth to you (see Box 9A).

The surest way to preserve the value of a solo practice is to take on an associate and work out a buy-sell arrangement. If association practice doesn't

BOX 9A
Are your practice assets worth this much?

Half the doctors surveyed by Medical Economics estimated the value of their practice assets at more than $40,000, not counting real estate. Nearly a fourth put the figure at $100,000 or over.

Amount of assets	% of MDs
$200,000 or more	7%
100,000 - 199,999	17
80,000 - 99,999	4
60,000 - 79,999	8
50,000 - 59,999	12
40,000 - 49,999	4
30,000 - 39,999	7
20,000 - 29,999	13
10,000 - 19,999	10
Less than $10,000	18

suit you, your best chance to realize its full worth is to sell it outright before its volume declines due to your advancing age or infirmity.

Advertising in state and local medical publications is often the first recourse for a doctor seeking a buyer. But you may waste a lot of time dealing with undesirable applicants. Sounding out house officers at hospitals often works better, as does spreading the word in the local medical community.

Faculties of medical schools and teaching hospitals are good but sometimes overlooked sources of leads to buyers. Medical meetings—specialty meetings in particular—are also good places to make contacts. If you're not going to a convention yourself, you can give a notice for posting to someone who will be there.

Success in attracting a buyer depends to a large degree on the specialty. A neurosurgeon might not have as much to offer as, say, a primary-care physician with a stable patient population. However, some specialty practices are marketable. The criterion is how much of the patient population originates with referrals from patients rather than other doctors.

Though the most likely candidate for a practice takeover is a fledgling physician, transactions between established practitioners are not uncommon. A retiring dermatologist sent out letters to other dermatologists in the community, describing his large following of revisiting patients, most of whom had been referred by other patients. He shortly received an inquiry from a dermatologist in the same area, and a deal resulted. The buyer was doing well enough to make a substantial down payment.

One advantage of selling to a doctor already in practice locally is greater assurance of the buyer's suitability and commitment to the community. You don't want him to decide after a short time that he'd be happier elsewhere.

Another way to find a buyer is through a professional-practice broker. His services may include appraising the assets, recommending methods of sale, arranging financing, and giving advice on the tax aspects of the sale and the handling of receivables. Brokers with nationwide listings generally charge the seller 10 to 12 percent of the sales price; firms covering smaller areas may charge as little as 5 or 6 percent. Most brokers say they like to allow about six months to find a buyer and complete a sale.

VALUATION OF PRACTICE ASSETS

Here are some guidelines to help you estimate the value of what you're selling. They don't apply to every situation, but they should give you a range.

Furnishings and equipment

Items less than two years old probably are worth from 65 to 75 percent of what you paid, provided they haven't been abused; older items fetch only about 25 percent. Some new items such as electronic office machines depreciate much faster than others because improved products are constantly being introduced.

Drugs and supplies

Typically you'll have about two months' stock of drugs and other medical supplies on hand. An offer of 50 to 75 percent of their value is acceptable.

Accounts receivable

You're likely to have two or three months' worth of gross charges on your books. If the total is $50,000 and your can collect 90 percent, that drops it to $45,000. The buyer will probably discount another 15 percent or so for collection expenses. Any bills over 90 days old for services not covered by health insurance may be further discounted by 30 percent. If the resulting offer is less than you think it should be, you can try to persuade the buyer to raise it by pointing out that receivables are a good way to maintain patient flow.

Office lease

When office rentals are rising, an unexpired lease can be worth a premium to the buyer—assuming that you're entitled to sublet. You might compute the value this way: 3 to 5 percent of the annual rental for each year you've had the lease times the number of years left. For example, if you make it 4 percent on a five-year lease at $10,000 a year with two years to run, the premium would be $2,400 ($400 x 3 x 2). When there's a lot of time left on the lease, and if the location is desirable and the rent is somewhat lower than usual for the area, the premium might be a bit higher.

Office improvements

If you rent your office and have made permanent improvements like built-in cabinets, special wiring and electrical connections, or lead shielding in the walls, they become the landlord's property unless your lease says otherwise. However, if the buyer would have to install them were they not already there, he should be willing to pay up to 50 percent of their cost.

Owned office

If you own the building in which you practice, there may be income and estate tax advantages to retaining it and renting the space to the buyer. You'll need advice from your tax consultant on this point, as well as from a knowledgeable realtor if you decide to sell.

Goodwill

Goodwill is harder to evaluate than a practice's tangible assets. It may include office location, retention of telephone numbers, and willingness of employees to stay on. But the most important factor is transferability of patients; and there's no way to predict with certainty how much of your following will stick with your successor.

One way to solve the problem is to use a formula based on the practice's recent income. Specialty affects the formula. "The practice of a family physician, internist, or pediatrician might sell for between 20 to 50 percent of the annual gross," says a Pennsylvania management consultant. "An OBG specialist might ask 30 percent. A high-demand practice, such as one in ophthalmology, might yield 50 to 100 percent of the gross."

A word of caution, however, from another consultant: "I always tell buyers to look at the bottom line. I've seen some practices that gross $300,000 and net $75,000, and others that gross $200,000 and net $120,000." (See Box 9B.) So your prospective buyer may insist on using a percentage of net.

Patient records

Charts that once sold for no more than 25 cents apiece may now go for $1 to $6 depending on specialty, consultants say. You must, of course, give patients the option of transferring their records to another physician instead of leaving them with your buyer. In some parts of the country, it's still rare for a separate valuation to be placed on records for ethical reasons. But their value is usually factored into the purchase price, even if it appears under other headings.

BOX 9B
Earnings ratios in various specialties

Median figures for practice net as a percentage of gross are shown.

Type of specialist	Earnings ratio
Anesthesiologists	82%
FPs	55
GPs	59
General surgeons	65
Internists	60
Neurologists	68
Neurosurgeons	72
OBGs	62
Ophthalmologists	62
Orthopedic surgeons	62
Otolaryngologists	61
Pediatricians	59
Plastic surgeons	61
Psychiatrists	76
Radiologists	86
Thoracic surgeons	71

Source: Medical Economics surveys.

Tax consequences

The way the sales contract values the various practice elements can have an important tax impact on both parties. For example, anything the seller gets for goodwill is taxed as a capital gain. But to the buyer, goodwill is a nondepreciable asset. He can't deduct anything for it since he doesn't use it up or wear it out. On the other hand, if the seller is paid for a covenant not to compete—that is, an agreement not to practice in the locality for a specific number of years—he must declare the money as ordinary income, whereas the buyer can amortize the payment over the life of the agreement. For example, if he pays $10,000 for a 10-year covenant, he can tax-deduct $1,000 a year.

Let's assume instead that the entire $10,000 is considered payment for goodwill. Then the buyer gets no current tax deduction, but the seller pays tax on only $4,000—40 percent of his capital gain. Obviously, compromises may be in order. (Box 9C summarizes the way various practice assets are taxed.)

Financing the purchase

Many prospective buyers find it hard to get bank financing, and even when they can get loans, they're charged formidable interest rates. So the selling

BOX 9C
How a practice sale is taxed

Here's a summary of how the various elements in a typical practice sale are treated for tax purposes by the seller and the buyer. Because of the complications that may arise, your tax adviser should be consulted before you sign the contract.

Professional asset	Seller's profit	Buyer's cost
Drugs and medical supplies	Ordinary income	Deductible expense in year purchased
Instruments and equipment	"Recaptured" depreciation is ordinary income; balance of profit is capital gain	Depreciable over remaining useful life
Clinical records	Value assigned (if any) is capital gain	May be depreciable if useful life can be reasonably estimated
Goodwill	Capital gain	Not deductible or depreciable*
Covenant not to compete	Ordinary income	Deductible as amortized expense over life of covenant
Professional building	Generally capital gain	Depreciable over useful life
Land	Capital gain	Not deductible or depreciable*

*If the buyer eventually sells the practice and fails to recover his investment, he can claim a loss.

doctor may have to become a lender. That's not all to the bad, however. If you take the sales price in installments with interest, you'll end up with more than you'd have received in a lump-sum payment arranged by the buyer through a bank, and the installment sale lets you spread the taxes over a span of years.

You should insist that the buyer put down as large an amount as he can afford, though, so that he won't be apt to walk away after the takeover. If the buyer defaults, repossessing the practice may be of little avail in recovering your loss. It may then be difficult or impossible to sell what's left of it.

You should also require the buyer to take out life and disability insurance naming you as beneficiary. Even a young and apparently healthy doctor can have a sudden illness or accident.

INFORMING YOUR HEIRS

If you're a solo operator, your heirs will need to know what to do about the assets and other matters in case you die owning the practice. Your letter or memo on the subject should cover these points:

□ *Sale of the practice*. Stress the necessity for fast action. The longer the sale is delayed, the less any goodwill you've built up will be worth. Be sure to tell your heirs whom to ask for help—for example, officials of local medical societies or medical schools, management consulting firms, and medical placement agencies.

□ *Unpaid accounts*. Your executor will normally take the necessary steps to collect such accounts, but your heirs should make sure that your office staff gives him full cooperation. Warn your heirs that many of those bills may not ever be collected.

□ *Office personnel*. Suggest appropriate severance pay arrangements for your office staff and advise your heirs whether any personnel should be kept on to wind up office business.

□ *Office property*. If there are likely to be problems in disposing of a building or lease, list the names of real estate agents and others who may be of assistance. (A standard lease will be binding on your estate unless you've negotiated an escape clause in the event of death. At a minimum, the lease should allow subletting.)

□ *Office equipment*. Suggest several colleagues or reliable dealers who may be helpful in disposing of your equipment. You might also suggest the possibility of donating the equipment to your hospital.

□ *Patients' records*. Advise your heirs to keep your patients' records readily available if the practice is not sold. After a year or so, the records can go into dead storage; they should not be destroyed until your heirs' attorney says it's safe. Paper records may be discarded after they've been transferred to microfilm, computer disk, or magnetic tape.

□ *Liability insurance*. Advise your heirs whether and how long to keep your liability insurance in force after your death. In most states, a malpractice action must be filed within one to three years unless the patient is a minor. Malpractice insurance usually can be dropped if the policy provides coverage indefinitely for events that occurred while the insurance was in effect. But if you have the claims-made type of insurance, coverage is available only if the policy is in effect when a claim is filed. So it may be necessary to buy a coverage extension to protect against any claim made after your death. You should talk this over with your insurance consultant and attorney to see what can be done to hold premiums down while still protecting your estate adequately. You should also preserve all of your malpractice insurance policy documents, even if you've dropped the coverage.

□ *Narcotics*. Warn your heirs to have the executor comply with government regulations. Records that should be kept for not less than two years include an inventory of all controlled substances on hand when the practice was terminated and duplicate copies of the official order forms used to obtain them. Any unused order forms should be returned to the local Drug Enforcement Administration office. DEA authorization is needed to dispose of existing controlled substances.

10

It may be better to give while you live

Whether or not you expect your spouse and children to inherit everything you own tax-free, lifetime gifts could play a very important and productive role in your estate plan. For one thing, you can't be absolutely certain that your estate will escape tax.

What if your spouse dies before you do, and the estate you then leave your children turns out to be larger than the tax-free amount? Or what if your surviving spouse's estate grows beyond the tax-free limit?

A judicious program of lifetime giving that guards against such uncertainties can lower the taxes for your heirs and may save you income taxes in the bargain. Perhaps most important, it offers you the satisfaction of seeing the effects of your bounty on those you care for.

GIFT TAX EXCLUSIONS

Large gifts made while you live are ordinarily subject to tax under the "unified rate schedule" applicable to your entire estate. As your gifts accumulate over the years, the tax due on them mounts up, but you don't actually pay anything until it exceeds the estate tax credit. Since the credit will cover as much as $600,000 in gifts, you may not have to pay tax while you live (see Box 10A for details). However, the more credit you use up this way, the less that's left to shield your estate from tax when you die.

The annual exclusion helps preserve the credit by freeing some of your gifts from tax altogether. It lets you give, tax-free, up to $10,000 a year apiece

BOX 10A
Gift tax rules

The rules are complex, so you'd do well to consult your adviser before making large gifts. Here's an example of how the gift tax operates:

In 1982, Dr. Franklin gave his adult daughter $40,000 cash. He filed a gift tax return (Form 709—see Appendix 5), which his wife also signed, consenting to the gift. That allowed him to claim a $20,000 exclusion for the year. According to the unified rate schedule (see Box 2C), the tax on the remaining $20,000 came to $3,800. Instead of paying this, he simply reduced his gift/estate tax credit by $3,800.

In 1983, Franklin gave his daughter $10,000 and his adult son $15,000. The $10,000 annual exclusion per individual covered the daughter's gift but only part of the son's, so Franklin had to file a return (Form 709-A). However, he owed no tax and didn't have to use up any more of his credit because the $5,000 balance on the son's gift was taken care of by the exclusion Mrs. Franklin could claim.

In 1984, Franklin set up a trust to hold insurance policies on his life, with his children as beneficiaries; the policies had a total cash value of $60,000. No annual exclusion could be claimed because this was a gift of a future interest. That brought his total taxable gifts to $80,000 ($60,000 in 1984 and $20,000 in 1982). The tax on $80,000 is $18,200. Note that Franklin must figure the tax on the entire amount rather than adding the tax on $20,000 ($3,800) to the tax on $60,000 (13,000) to get $16,800. Although Franklin had to file a return, he still paid no tax, thanks to the credit.

If Franklin dies in 1989, say, without making any more taxable gifts, his estate will be increased by the $80,000 of lifetime gifts, and the full credit—$192,800—can be used to reduce the combined gift/estate tax. So Franklin's prior gift tax returns don't change the end result, but they do provide a record to help figure it. Also, there are penalties for failure to file a gift tax return.

Although you don't have to report a gift that comes within the $10,000 annual exclusion, it may be wise to file a return anyway if the gift is likely to appreciate in value substantially. For gift tax purposes, the IRS has only three years to dispute the valuation on your return; if they don't challenge it, they've tacitly approved it. Let's say you die many years from now, and your estate tax return is audited. The IRS could claim the gift was worth a good deal more than $10,000 when you made it. Although the IRS isn't bound by the uncontested gift tax return, it strengthens the executor's position. Without it, he might be hard put to win the argument after the long time lapse. It may also be prudent to get an independent appraisal at the time of the gift.

---

to any number of persons, or $20,000 apiece if your spouse consents to the gift. You may make gifts of any size to your spouse tax-free, but they may later be taxed as part of *her* estate.

Take a married doctor with three grown children who expects to leave an estate of $1.5 million. If he adopts the standard bypass trust described in Chapter 2, the children will ultimately get $1.2 million tax-free. The estate tax on the remaining $300,000 would amount to $114,000. Suppose that, with his spouse's consent, the doctor gives each child $100,000 this year. That would reduce his taxable estate by $60,000—three times the $20,000 exclusion; the

$240,000 balance would be added back at his death, eventually triggering a tax of $90,600. But if he spreads out the gifts over five years at the rate of $20,000 annually per child, the whole $300,000 will be permanently removed from the estate, saving the children $114,000.

The above example assumes that, in making the yearly gifts to his children, the doctor gives them a "present interest"—i.e., the right to "the immediate use, possession, or enjoyment" of the gift. If the right commences at a future date, the gift doesn't qualify for the exclusion. As explained later, this distinction can have significant tax consequences.

In addition to the normal annual exclusion of a $10,000 (or $20,000) gift, there's an *unlimited* exclusion for gifts of tuition or medical-expense payments. Generally speaking, such payments aren't taxable as gifts if you make them for your dependents, so the exclusion isn't needed there. But suppose you'd like to finance the education of your grandchild or someone else who's *not* your dependent. If you give the money to him or his parents, the gift is taxable, subject to the normal annual exclusion. But if you pay the tuition directly to the school, it's tax-free without limit. Let's say tuition is $8,500 a year, and expenses for books, living quarters, and other expenses are another $4,000. You can give the whole $12,500 tax-free; the tuition is covered by the special exclusion, and the rest by the normal exclusion.

The medical-gift exclusion likewise applies only to payments made directly to whoever provides the services. This too is unlimited, except that insurance reimbursements to the patient or anyone else must be subtracted.

As already mentioned, there's no need to worry about exclusions when it comes to gifts between spouses. It's logical that they shouldn't be subject to gift tax, since everything one spouse leaves the other is tax-free until the survivor dies. However, such gifts may still have tax advantages. Take the case of a doctor and his wife who are both well along in years. The doctor's will divides his $900,000 estate between her and the children so that if he dies first, the children will benefit from two tax credits and Uncle Sam will probably get nothing. But if the doctor outlives his wife, the maximum $600,000 credit won't prevent estate tax at his death. The couple could pare down the estate by yearly gifts of $20,000 to each child. They should bear in mind, though, that this means giving away money they may eventually need if both live many years longer.

But they don't have to part with any of it. The doctor can guard against his wife's premature death by making a gift of $300,000 to her. Then, if she died first, the money would go to the children tax-free; her will could leave it to them outright or in trust with the doctor as income beneficiary.* If his assets keep increasing while his wife lives, he can make additional gifts to build her estate up to the maximum covered by the tax credit.

---

*In a community-property state, the wife would automatically own half the community property and could dispose of it in her will. It's important to determine just what property would be covered, since community property is defined differently in various states.

GIFTS TO MINORS

Giving large amounts of cash or other assets directly to a young or immature child is usually impractical and may be legally restricted by state law. There are a number of suitable alternatives, some of which may save income taxes as well as estate taxes:

Account in your name as custodian for a child

This type of account, permitted in almost every state, lets you maintain complete control over the funds deposited until the child reaches legal age. Formerly, control of such accounts passed to the child at age 21, but since the vote was granted to 18-year-olds, most state legislatures have accordingly amended the laws that govern these accounts. Generally, custodial accounts can include cash, securities, annuity contracts, and insurance policies, but your state may not allow other types of assets—e.g., real estate, royalties, partnership interests—to go into them.

Since the child owns the assets, whatever they earn will normally be taxable to him and not to you. Like any other taxpayer, he's entitled to an exemption each year, so the account could earn up to that much and still be tax-free. You can continue to claim the child as a dependent as long as you furnish more than 50 percent of his support and he is under 19 or a full-time student.

To get the income tax breaks, make sure the earnings aren't credited to you. Give the bank your child's Social Security number instead of your own. If he doesn't have a number, you can get one for him by filing an application form available at post offices and banks.

If you die before control of the account passes to the child, its value will be included in your estate and subject to estate tax. Also, the income from the account is taxable to you if you use it to support the child, and in some states support includes college expenses. Of course, once the child is of age, he can use the funds for expenses without adverse tax consequences to you. Your contributions to the account are taxable gifts, but the annual exclusion applies.

Account in the name of a third person as custodian for a child

You can also open a custodial account with your spouse or someone else as custodian. In most states, any adult, bank, or trust company will do. If you have a relative or friend who will serve for nothing, fine. Otherwise, the fee charged by a bank or trust company may cancel out some of the tax savings.

By keeping your name off the account, you get the income tax break and you also remove the assets from your estate. (The annual exclusion applies to your gifts.) But even though someone other than you is custodian, the income from the account will be taxable to you if it's used to support your child. And if you name someone else as custodian, only he can withdraw what you've contributed, so you've parted company with those assets forever. Obviously it's important to choose a custodian of integrity and judgment who's likely to live and carry out his responsibility until the child is of age.

Caution: Don't confuse custodial accounts with a so-called Totten trust—an account in your name, in trust for the child. This isn't a true trust and won't save you any taxes. The earnings from the account are taxable to you, whether you withdraw them or not. Since the contributions belong to you, they're not taxable as gifts, but any assets in the account when you die are part of your estate. However, they'll go to the child automatically after your death, with no probate proceedings or administrative expenses.

Irrevocable trust

Unlike a custodial account, there are generally no restrictions on the type of assets you can put into a trust for minors. To prevent its assets from being taxed as part of your estate, the trust must be irrevocable and you shouldn't be a trustee. The annual exclusion applies to gifts if the beneficiary gets the trust when he comes of age; that can be 21, even if adulthood in your state is 18.

If you want the trust to operate beyond age 21, you can still claim the annual exclusion provided the trust document gives the beneficiary either the power to terminate the trust at 21 or else the power to withdraw up to $10,000 (or $20,000) of your contributions when made. You can allow him only 30 or 60 days to exercise the power before it lapses, and you can hope he'll be sensible enough not to use it, so that the trust can continue as you wish.

Like income from a custodial account, trust income isn't taxable to you unless it's used to discharge your support obligation to a beneficiary. Instead, the income will be taxed at the trust's or the beneficiary's low rate. Thus, you can get all the tax breaks of a custodial account plus a trust's flexibility, stability, and other advantages (see Chapter 4). This combination of desirable features may well outweigh the fact that the trust arrangement will be more expensive, especially if you appoint a professional trustee.

Short-term trust

This device—also known as a Clifford trust—is often used to establish a fund for a child's college education or some similar limited purpose. You set up a trust that names your child as beneficiary of the income only. After a period of time—the law requires a minimum of 10 years and a day—the principal comes back to you. Obviously, such an arrangement calls for more initial capital than a regular trust to provide the fund your beneficiary will need, since you intend to give him just the income. But the more time you have to build up the fund, the smaller that drawback is.

The mechanics of a short-term trust resemble those for any other trust. A lawyer draws up the agreement; you name a trustee—yourself, if you prefer—to handle the money. The trustee can either pay out the income or bank it until the minor needs it.

Because the principal reverts to you, a short-term trust doesn't directly reduce the size of your estate. Its advantage lies in its ability to shift income from your high bracket to your beneficiary's low one. As with a custodial account, the earnings on the trust assets are taxable to you only if used to pay for your child's support as defined by state law. However, capital gains from the sale of the assets may be taxed to you, so it's usually desirable to fund the trust with income-type investments like bonds.

Since you're giving away the income, its value is subject to gift tax, but the $10,000 annual exclusion applies. As the IRS figures it, the value of 10 years' income equals 61.45 percent of the principal (a 10 percent interest rate is assumed). That means you can contribute $16,275 to a 10-year trust without paying gift tax—61.45 percent of $16,275 equals $10,000. Actually, a $16,275 lump sum invested for 10 years at prevailing interest rates might yield upwards of $25,000, but the excess interest wouldn't be taxable as a gift.

Bear in mind that you can double the tax-free contribution if your spouse joins in the gift. Also, if the trust is to last longer than 10 years, you can increase the tax-free amount by making gifts in more than one year, because the annual exclusion would apply separately to each (see Box 10B). For instance, with a 14-year trust, a married couple could put in a total of nearly $150,000 spread over several years. (The last contribution would have to be made while the trust still had more than 10 years to run, in order to preserve the income tax advantages.)

Once you establish the trust, it must run until the term ends, unless the beneficiary dies sooner. If you think you might need some of the capital before the trust terminates, you can give the trustee the power to lend you money at market-interest rates. In that case, you should name an independent trustee, not your spouse or a relative.

If you die during the period the trust is in operation, the assets will count in your estate, but at reduced value, since they remain tied up until the trust period expires. Normally, your death won't terminate the trust, but you can set it up to do so, provided your life expectancy is 10 years or more at the time you contribute the funds. That would give your heirs access to the trust capital if you died prematurely.

Note: A short-term trust can also provide income tax savings when established for an adult dependent, such as an aging parent. The tax result may be even better than with a minor, since the issue of your legal obligation to furnish support is unlikely to arise. Second, an elderly trust beneficiary is apt to have more exemptions and deductions than a child and can therefore receive more income without paying tax.

BOX 10B
Annual exclusion for gifts of trust income

As explained in this chapter, the annual exclusion applies to the "present value" of a stream of future income from principal contributed to a short-term or spousal remainder trust. For a given number of years, the table shows the amount of principal that will yield an income stream with a present value of $10,000. A married couple can contribute twice the amounts shown without owing gift tax.

Years of income	Amount of principal*
20	$ 11,746
19	11,954
18	12,193
17	12,466
16	12,782
15	13,147
14	13,575
13	14,078
12	14,676
11	15,396
10	16,275
9	17,364
8	18,744
7	20,541
6	22,961
5	26,380
4	31,547
3	40,211
2	57,619
1	110,000

*Based on the IRS assumption of a 10 percent interest rate.

Spousal remainder trust

Suppose you don't have 10 years to build up a child's education fund via a short-term trust, or you don't want to tie up your capital that long. You can get around the 10-year requirement if the trust principal goes to someone other than you—to your spouse, for instance. Then you can choose whatever trust termination date suits you best.*

If your spouse gets the trust remainder—i.e., the principal you contributed—it's exempt from gift tax. As with a standard short-term trust, you're not

---

*If you live in a community-property state, make sure the assets you put into the trust are your separate property. Because your spouse would be half-owner of community property contributed to the trust, the 10-year minimum would apply if the trust assets revert to her at expiration.

Estate planning strategies for physicians

taxed on the income, and its present value is a taxable gift to which the annual exclusion applies. However, the fund you can contribute tax-free will be greater than with a 10-year trust, assuming a shorter duration. For example, with a four-year trust, a couple could put in as much as $63,000, compared to around $32,500 with a 10-year trust. That's because the present value of four years' income is less than that of 10 years' income.

GIVING AWAY POTENTIAL GAINS

If lifetime gifts can produce estate tax benefits for your heirs, you can magnify these benefits by giving away assets that are likely to appreciate. Dr. Gray, for example, put up $50,000 of capital to start a medical computer service a few years ago. Today he estimates the company is worth $100,000, and its value may well grow to $500,000 in another five or 10 years' time. By then, the rest of Gray's assets may be large enough to make the entire $500,000 taxable when his three children inherit the estate. If so, the tax cost will come to around $190,000 or more. One ray of sunshine: If the company is sold for $500,000 postmortem, there'll be no capital-gains tax to pay, because the heirs' cost basis will be the value at Gray's death.

Suppose, however, that the doctor gives his stock in the company to the children now, when it's worth only $100,000. This would remove the future $400,000 appreciation from his estate. And the annual gift-tax exclusion would eliminate the present $100,000 if Gray spread the gifts over two years and made them jointly with his wife (it doesn't matter whether she's a co-owner or not). The children would escape all of the estate tax, though they would have to pay income tax on the capital gain if they sold the stock. Their cost basis would be the same as Gray's—$50,000—so the maximum tax would be $90,000 (20 percent of $450,000), a net saving of $100,000 over the estate tax.

Recapitalization

If any of the children are minors, Gray can give his stock to them using a custodial account or trust as previously described. But in that case—or even if all are adults—he may want to make sure of retaining control of the company himself. Instead of giving away the common stock, he can "recapitalize"—replace it with two classes of stock, a nonvoting common and a voting preferred, say. Gray would then hold the preferred and give the nonvoting common away. The value of the preferred would be fixed; therefore, any future appreciation in the company's worth would accrue to holders of the common, Gray's children.*

---

*If a company's current value is high, it's often desirable to assign most of it to the preferred, so as to avoid paying gift tax on the common. The preferred stock should bear a substantial dividend rate, payable cumulatively.

Certain formalities must be strictly observed in order not to jeopardize the estate tax advantages and avoid possible income tax problems. For example, if some of the stock is sold during Gray's lifetime, the profit might conceivably be taxed as ordinary income. Consequently, a recapitalization should be undertaken only with the guidance and supervision of an attorney versed in securities law. (The hazards are fewer if the two classes of stock are issued at the time the corporation is formed.)

Bargain or installment sale

What if you're satisfied to give away the potential appreciation of an asset, yet want to retain some or all of its current value yourself? In a recapitalization, that value can be assigned to the voting stock which you'll own. But suppose the asset is a parcel of real estate rather than a stock company. Say you paid $25,000 for land outside of town that's currently worth $75,000 and should increase perhaps fourfold when urban development reaches the area in the next decade. To keep that gain in the family but out of your estate, you can sell the property to an heir—your son, for instance. If you sell it for $75,000, there's no gift. If your son can't afford that much, you have two choices: You can take less, in which case the difference is a gift subject to tax. Or you can take payment in installments.

If the total sale price is more than your $25,000 cost, you'll be taxed on the capital gain. By law, installment payments must include a reasonable amount allocated to interest, taxable to you as ordinary income. Even if you later forgive the installment payments as they come due, the interest will be taxable income imputed to you (see Box 10C). Moreover, a canceled payment is a gift, although the annual exclusion applies and may shield it from tax. Evidently, a bargain or installment sale of an appreciating asset won't eliminate taxes altogether, but they may often amount to far less than the future estate tax saved.

Private annuity

This can be looked upon as a more sophisticated version of an installment sale. It may be particularly useful in the case of a doctor with assets that have already appreciated a great deal.

Dr. White, for instance, owns a $600,000 apartment building that has a cost basis of only $100,000. Future appreciation figures to be modest by comparison. If White gives the property away, not only will there be a sizable gift tax, but the recipient will be stuck with a $500,000 capital-gains tax liability as well. Seemingly, White's heirs would be better off if the property remained in his estate. The estate tax then promises to be little greater than the gift tax, assuming only moderate appreciation between now and White's death; and the tax liability for all the capital gain in his lifetime will be wiped out.

BOX 10C
Low-rate family loans

If you charge less than the market rate of interest on a loan to a family member (or other individual), the difference is a gift to the borrower. Moreover, you're liable for income tax on the interest you forgo. The market rate is the average yield on Treasury securities with a term comparable to that of the loan. Thus, if you lend your son $100,000 for a year at 6 percent when the market rate is 10 percent, you've made him a gift of $4,000. There might be no gift tax because of the annual exclusion, but you'd have to report $10,000 of interest on your income tax return even though he pays you only $6,000. By the same token, on **his** tax return, he could claim $10,000 of interest paid if he itemizes deductions.

The main reason for these rules is to discourage high-bracket taxpayers from shifting income by lending funds at little or no interest to low-bracket family members for investment. If the borrowed money isn't used to buy or carry income-producing assets, no interest will be imputed for income tax purposes on loan balances of $10,000 or less.* Even if the balance is as much as $100,000, the imputed interest can't be more than the borrower's net investment income. So you can, for instance, make a sizable interest-free loan to your son to set him up in practice without incurring much income tax on phantom interest. The forgone interest is still a gift, but is apt to be less than the annual exclusion. The loan itself must be repaid, however, to avoid a possible gift tax on the principal.

Be careful of imputed interest when you make an installment sale, whether to a family member or anyone else. If the interest rate stated in the contract is less than the rate prescribed by law or regulations, part of the sales price may be allocated to interest and taxed as ordinary income rather than capital gain.

* In figuring the total outstanding, you must combine amounts lent by you and your spouse to the borrower and his spouse.

But suppose that White transfers the building to his heirs in return for a life income equal to the property's actuarial value—that is, the equivalent of the amount an insurance company would contract to pay him for a $600,000 single premium. If the formalities are observed, the transaction is a sale, not a gift, so there's no gift tax to pay; and since White no longer owns the property, there'll be no estate tax on it when he dies. For income tax purposes, each payment White receives consists of three parts: taxable capital gain, taxable interest, and untaxable return of capital.

If White doesn't spend all of the annuity income he gets, what's left will add to his estate, but assuming the annuity is straight life, it will have no remaining value at his death. His heirs won't be saddled with his past capital gain and will be able to claim depreciation deductions based on the $600,000 sale price of the property. However, they'd have to reduce their basis if White died prematurely.

In the right circumstances, a private-annuity arrangement may yield worthwhile savings on both capital-gains taxes and gift/estate taxes. Unfortunately, it stands to work best if the annuitant's lifespan turns out to be shorter than statistically expected. That could make it psychologically undesirable despite the possible economic benefits. (Also, if the annuitant is seriously ill when the arrangement is made, the IRS might question its validity.)

Remainder interests

One obstacle to the use of a private-annuity or installment-sale arrangement as a means of removing capital-gains property from your estate is that the recipient is required to make periodic payments to you even if you don't want them and they work a hardship on him. This can be especially vexing if the property is not income-producing—a valuable art collection, for example. The recipient might raise the money by selling off the assets, but this may not be feasible or desirable. Also, if you'd made an installment sale to your child, you could be liable for capital-gains tax if the resale took place within two years.

Some estate planners suggest a gift of a remainder interest as a solution. It might work this way: Suppose a doctor who owns an art collection appraised at $500,000 signs it over to his children now, but retains the right to keep and enjoy it for the next 15 years. How much is the gift worth? Not $500,000, but the present value of $500,000 assuming a 10 percent annual rate of return for 15 years; that's roughly $120,000 (see Box 10D). Even if the collection doubles in value during the 15 years, the additional $500,000 won't be subject to gift or estate tax.

In essence, the doctor will have given away a $1 million asset while paying gift tax on just $120,000. The figure can't be further reduced by the annual exclusion because it doesn't cover gifts of a future interest. But that's of little consequence in view of the overall tax saving.

An important caveat: The IRS might argue that the gift will not be completed until the collection actually passes into the children's possession, so that tax is due on its full value then. The IRS case would be strengthened if the doctor's life expectancy was less than 15 years, because gifted property in which you retain an interest for life must be included in your estate.

For instance, you can't escape tax by transferring your home to your children if there's an understanding that you'll continue to live there until death. However, that rule doesn't apply if you *sell* the remainder interest for what it's worth instead of giving it away. So an installment sale of such an interest might achieve your objective in some cases. Obviously, arrangements of this kind call for expert tax guidance.

CHARITABLE GIFTS

Though motivated by a spirit of generosity, sizable contributions to charity should be as carefully thought out as any other element in your estate plan. Properly handled, donations can save income tax in your lifetime and estate tax after death.

BOX 10D
Valuing gifts of income or "remainders"

If you give ownership of an asset to someone while keeping the right to its income or use for a period of time, what is the value of the gift? The answer depends on the length of the period, as shown in the table. For example, if a doctor puts a rental property in trust for his son and retains the income from it for five years, the present value of his retained interest is approximately 38 percent of the property's worth, and the remainder interest is 100 minus 38, or 62 percent. So if the property is worth $100,000 today, the value of the remainder for gift tax purposes is $62,000. If the doctor retained the income for 15 years instead of five, his interest would be worth more, $76,000, and the remainder correspondingly less, $24,000.

Such an arrangement, known as a "grantor income trust," not only reduces the gift tax but also removes future appreciation of the property from the doctor's estate. However, it means that he'll be taxed on the income during the trust period. The higher your gift/estate tax bracket, the more advantageous this type of trust is likely to be.

Two further points: The value of an income interest for life—called a "life estate" — is measured by the life expectancy of the person for whom the interest is created. But any property you own in which you retain a life estate will count as part of your estate at death, even if you've given away the remainder interest. The same principle applies if you retain only a limited income interest but die before the period ends.

Number of years	Value of income*	Value of "remainder"*
5	38%	62%
10	61	39
15	76	24
20	85	15
25	91	9
30	94	6
35	96	4
40	98	2
45	99	1

* Based on the IRS assumption of a 10 percent interest rate. For a term of years not shown here, see Appendix 4, Table B.

Donating appreciated property

Do you have assets that have gone up in value since you acquired them? In most cases, by donating them to charity, you not only can deduct the current fair market value as a charitable contribution, but you also escape tax on the capital gain. There's a limit to the amount you can deduct each year this way—30 percent of your adjusted gross income (that's your total income less all subtractions except personal deductions and exemptions). If you donate more than the limit, you may carry the nondeductible excess over to future years.

As pointed out in this chapter, lifetime gifts of business interests may reduce the tax on your estate. Such gifts can sometimes save you income taxes, too. For instance, family members may be given co-ownership of income-producing assets or enterprises other than your medical practice. (Chapter 8 discusses the use of corporations and trust-leasebacks for this purpose.) Another possibility is to form a partnership with, say, a son who is starting his own business. This may produce some income tax deductions for you, while giving him a leg up.

Suppose that, in the first year, the partnership nets $5,000 before paying your son a salary of $25,000. All told, the partnership is $20,000 in the red, and each partner can deduct half of that. What if the business starts making more money than it's paying out in salary and other expenses, so it has a gain to report? The partnership can forestall that problem by giving your son raises, as long as they're commensurate with the services he performs. The partnership may eventually generate taxable profit anyway, but even then only half of that profit will have to be reported on your return. (Remember, though, income from your services can't be split with a passive partner.)

Donating principal but keeping income

A charitable remainder trust allows a charity to accept a gift of property from you now and pay you—or another named beneficiary—income in exchange. You can specify any annual return from 5 percent up. You'll specify a low yield if you want the biggest charitable deduction—which you claim for the year you make the contribution. That's because the deduction is based on the charity's remainder interest in the gift; the more income you take, the less the remainder interest will be worth to the charity.

The remainder value is figured on an actuarial basis, meaning that the longer your life expectancy is, the less the gift is worth. Depending on your age, you may choose to increase the gift's value by limiting the number of years you'll draw income.

There are two types of charitable remainder trusts: unitrusts and annuities. With a unitrust, you're paid a fixed percentage of the trust fund's value each year. For example, if you specify 6 percent and contribute $100,000 of assets, you won't necessarily get $6,000 every year. If the assets increase in value to $120,000, you'd get $7,200; if they decline to $80,000, you'd get only $4,800. However, you can provide that the unitrust must make up the difference from principal currently or from future earnings retroactively, as you prefer. Thus you can, to some extent, tailor the payout to suit your anticipated tax and financial situation.

Annuities provide you a guaranteed fixed income, in contrast to the variable return you might get from a unitrust. The annuity income is based on the initial fair market value of the donated assets and is apt to be less than you'd get from an insurance company. Compensating for that is the tax write-off you get in the year you make the contribution.

You also benefit from an immediate income tax deduction for donations to a unitrust. Suppose you're 60 and planning to retire soon. You put $50,000 into a unitrust that will pay you an annual 8 percent of the principal for life. The IRS actuarial tables will show you're entitled to a deduction of more than $15,000.

The tax benefit may reach dramatic proportions if you make your donation when your earnings and taxes are high but defer getting trust income until you're older. This boosts the remainder value because the charity has the use of your money for a long time without giving you anything in return. Let's say that in your early 50s you put $50,000 into a deferred gift annuity that will pay you $5,000 annually starting at 65. In the year of the donation, you'd get a deduction of more than $30,000.

You can make only a one-time contribution to a charitable annuity trust. So if you plan to make a series of gifts, you'll do better to set up a unitrust.

What kind of assets can you use to fund a charitable remainder trust? Charities prefer cash, but they'll accept securities or other salable assets. Where possible, donate appreciated assets. Then both your tax deduction and the income you get will be based on current market value, and as explained above, you'll owe no capital-gains tax. And neither will the charity if it chooses to sell the assets.

Instead of setting up a trust of your own, you can contribute a remainder interest to a pooled income fund established by a charity. Many such funds accept minimum donations as low as $5,000. They operate like mutual funds. A professional manager invests the pooled donations in diverse securities, and the donors share whatever returns the investments provide. The big difference, of course, is that you can't withdraw your principal; when you die, it goes to the charity. Your tax deduction is the actuarial value of your donation based on your life expectancy when you make it.

Donating property income but retaining remainder interest

The mirror image of a charitable remainder trust is what's known as a charitable lead trust or front-end trust. You give away the income produced by the trust property to a charity for a specified term of years, after which the property goes to the person or persons you name. With a front-end trust, only the value of the remainder interest in the property is subject to tax as part of your estate. That value is fixed at the time of the donation and is unaffected by any future appreciation of the property. There are usually no income tax benefits to the donor of a charitable front-end trust (you pay no tax on the trust income and therefore can't claim a deduction), but the gift/estate tax savings can be very sizable for large estates.

Private charities

A private charity gives you more control over who benefits from your generosity. Not that a private charity can single out a particular person for its help, but it can narrow the range of its giving. For example, you can't set up a private charity solely to provide a scholarship for a neighbor's child. But you *can* set one up to benefit students in your town who want to attend the medical school you graduated from.

You face a lot of red tape in this form of gift-giving. You have to incorporate a foundation, then get IRS approval of the foundation's tax-exempt status, keep flawless financial records, and make sure the recipients meet criteria called for in the charity's charter. That costs a good deal of money for lawyers and accountants. But if you join other doctors in making sizable contributions, you have a charity that gives you not only deductions but some discretion as to who benefits from your largesse.

Bear in mind that you can't deduct more than 20 percent of your adjusted gross income for the year when you contribute to a private charity. And if you go beyond that limit, you can't carry the excess over to future years.

Testamentary vs. lifetime donations

An obvious advantage to making charitable gifts in your will rather than while still alive is that you continue to have full control of the money and can change your mind if your financial needs or charitable objectives change. There's no limit on the size of the charitable deduction an estate can claim. As in life, your will can set up trusts providing income for individual heirs and giving the remainder to charity or vice versa. In some cases, the estate tax saving from a charitable gift can yield more income for your heirs than they would get if the gift were not made and the tax paid. However, the advantages of testamentary gifts must be weighed against the tax and other economic benefits of lifetime gifts, as well as the personal satisfaction you may get from them.

11

If you're unmarried or divorced

Dr. Abbott and Dr. Blake both figure to die as millionaires. When the Abbott children inherit their million, none of it will go for estate taxes. But the government will take at least $153,000 of the Blake children's inheritance. Why? Simply because Abbott is married and Blake isn't. If you're single—never married or else divorced or widowed—your heirs, whoever they may be, are likely to face similar discrimination. And that doesn't apply only to million-dollar estates. Your heirs will pay at least $75,000 on an $800,000 estate if you die single.

Not that the law is prejudiced against unmarried men and women as such. It isn't. But it does allow married couples to arrange their estates in tax-saving ways that aren't open to singles. For example, a married couple can split their estate to give their heirs the benefit of two tax credits, for a potential saving of several hundred thousand dollars on the tax a single doctor's estate would owe (see Box 11A). The couple also gets double the exclusion for annual gifts that an unmarried doctor can claim. Fortunately, proper planning may help the single MD overcome those handicaps to an appreciable extent.

GIVE THE RIGHT WAY AT THE RIGHT TIME

Whether you're married or single, the simplest way to cut taxes on your estate is to reduce its size by giving your heirs some of it during your lifetime. True, a doctor with no spouse can give only $10,000 a year per person free of gift

BOX 11A
Estate tax when you die single

A married couple can pass on a joint estate of up to $1.2 million tax free, but the tab on a single doctor's estate will quickly mount if he leaves more than $600,000. Planning can help slow it down.

Taxable estate*	Amount of tax
$ 600,000	$ 0
700,000	37,000
800,000	75,000
900,000	114,000
1,000,000	153,000
1,100,000	194,000
1,200,000	235,000

* After deducting administrative expenses, debts, and charitable donations. Death occurs in 1987 or later.

tax. But if that person were, say, a man with a wife and two children, the doctor could give the family as much as $40,000 annually untaxed.

One disadvantage of cash gifts is that you'll have paid income tax on the money beforehand. That's especially vexing for single doctors because they're likely to be in a higher bracket than married ones. If you're in the 50 percent bracket and your investments yield, say, 12 percent pretax, you need the income from $167,000 worth of assets to give away $10,000. It would be better for your beneficiary to own the assets and pay tax on the income in his lower bracket. If you don't want to give up your capital permanently, you can put assets into a short-term trust and get the principal back after 10 years.

As explained in Chapter 10, this arrangement allows you to escape income tax on the trust earnings, but the income you're giving away is subject to gift tax. That's in addition to the estate tax payable on the trust principal which reverts to you.

For the typical married doctor whose estate will be split between his spouse and children, the extra gift/estate tax resulting from the trust is likely to amount to little or nothing. But for a single MD, the added tax could be substantial. He can save his heirs that money if he can afford to give away the principal permanently. Then there'd be no taxable gift of income, and the tax on the gift of principal would be the same in life as at death.*

You don't have to give the principal outright to the beneficiary in order to save taxes. You might, for instance, fund a trust to finance a child's educa-

---

*If you've used up your gift/estate tax credit, the lifetime gift would be less advantageous because you'd have to pay tax on it currently. There's still an income tax saving and probably also an estate tax saving because the income won't accumulate in the doctor's estate.

Estate planning strategies for physicians

tion, with some or all of the principal going to him or her after graduation, upon marriage, or at some specified age. You can even have the income or the principal go to someone else—other than yourself—when the child is through school or established in a career. Provided the trust is irrevocable, there's almost no limit to the flexibility you can build into it and still not be liable for gift tax on the income.

In general, you do better to give away assets that have the potential to appreciate in value but haven't done so yet. Then only the value of the assets at the time the gift is made would be subject to gift/estate tax. Techniques for making such gifts are described in Chapter 10.

It's usually not a good idea, however, to put an asset in joint name with a prospective heir, figuring that you'll control it while you live and still save estate tax on half the appreciation when you die. Unless your heir could prove he contributed to the purchase of the jointly owned asset, its full value would be counted in your estate if you died first. (This rule doesn't apply to gifts between spouses.) There would be a saving in probate costs, though, since the asset would go directly to the co-owner. And if the asset yields income, you would be taxed only on half of it, so there could be a saving during your lifetime as well.

Finally, avoid giving away an asset with no growth potential if it's worth less than you paid for it, because then the recipient's cost basis is the market value at the time of the gift. That means neither he nor you get any tax benefit from the capital loss. So consider selling the asset and giving the cash instead.

SHELTER YOUR HOME FROM THE IRS

For understandable reasons, married couples usually want their homes to go to the surviving spouse when the other dies. But it's good planning for a single doctor to remove such a big-ticket asset from the taxable estate. Take care how you do that, though, or you may saddle your heirs with a needless tax burden.

For example, 57-year-old Dr. Dorman, whose wife died recently, owns a home now worth $200,000 and has more than $600,000 of other assets. In another 10 years, if he lives that long, the house may well be valued at $300,000. The estate tax on that would come to at least $114,000, but there would be no capital-gains tax, even though Dorman originally paid only $75,000 for the house.

Dorman could save his heirs—his daughter and her husband—$39,000 in estate tax by giving them title to the house now, since the present value of the gift is $200,000. But he would also be giving them his capital-gains tax liability, because that's based on what the gift cost the donor, not its present value. Ultimately, the gift could end up costing Dorman's heirs more in income tax than it would save in estate tax.

Dorman has a more attractive option: He can sell the house to the couple at market value, taking back a large mortgage and paying them a fair rental

Any tax on the profit from the sale of your home is postponed when you replace it with a more expensive one. If you've done that several times over the years, you're likely to have accumulated a sizable capital-gains tax liability. This may complicate your plans for disposing of your present home. However, you may be eligible for a once-in-a-lifetime break that lets you exclude up to $125,000 of your home-sale gain from tax. To qualify, you must be at least 55 and have lived in the house for three of the last five years prior to the sale. (A married couple qualifies if they own the house jointly and either is at least 55.)

Note that this is an exclusion, not a postponement. If you take advantage of it, you'll never pay tax on the excluded gain. But think carefully, because this is a one-shot deal. It generally makes sense to keep postponing tax until your gain approaches the $125,000 limit. If your gain is over the limit when you sell, you may also be able to postpone the excess. For example: You make a $135,000 profit on the sale of your home for $300,000 and buy a condominium apartment. If your new home costs at least $175,000 ($300,000 minus the $125,000 exclusion), the tax on your remaining $10,000 gain is postponed.

Finally, suppose you're getting along in years and have used up your exclusion. You want to move from your present home but not replace it with another of at least equal value. Consider renting it out instead of selling at a profit. If you choose to do that, you won't have to pay any capital-gains tax while you live, and neither will your heirs.

---

while he continues to live in it. The sale removes the house from the estate, and the outgoing rent, escalating with inflation, will keep the incoming mortgage payments from restoring the home's value to the estate. The heirs' cost basis is $200,000, so they escape tax on the doctor's $125,000 capital gain. But so does he, because he can claim the one-time exclusion available to homeowners over 55 (see Box 11B).

It's important to handle the sale and lease as formal business transactions in order to withstand IRS scrutiny. For instance, the mortgage interest rate must not be less than the minimum prescribed by law. The doctor has to pay tax on the interest, but the new owners can deduct it and other expenses, including depreciation, if they exceed the rental income.

One hitch in this arrangement: Dorman might die before his daughter and son-in-law paid off the mortgage. To guard against that, the terms of sale can provide that the couple's obligation ceases with his death. The IRS might well contend that the cancellation is a bequest, though the Tax Court has ruled otherwise in a case involving business property. But even if the unpaid mortgage balance is taxable as part of Dorman's estate, it will be less than the current value of the house.

Alternatively, if Dorman isn't set on remaining in the house, he can sell it to a non-family member, claim the over-55 exclusion on his capital gain, and use the $200,000 proceeds to purchase stock in a cooperative apartment building. Each year, assuming the co-op permits, he then gives his daughter and her husband a $20,000 share free of gift tax. Meanwhile, he occupies the co-op apartment, pays the maintenance fee, and as part owner tax-deducts a portion of the fee allocable to mortgage interest and property taxes. Eventually, the full value of the co-op will be out of Dorman's estate, with no adverse income tax consequences to himself or his heirs.

WARD OFF A SECOND ESTATE TAX

Dr. Elmont is fond of his sister Clara's two boys, but he's inadvertently playing them a dirty trick. His will leaves everything to Clara. Elmont's mother, his only other living relative, is supported by his father's large trust fund, which will also go to Clara when Mrs. Elmont dies. All this means that the estate Clara will leave her children stands to be heavily taxed.

Dr. Elmont can do his nephews a big favor by leaving his estate to them instead. To provide for Clara, in case he dies before his mother, his estate can be placed in a trust, with the income—and part of the principal, if she needs it—going to Clara during her lifetime. The legacy will, of course, be taxed at the doctor's death if it exceeds the exemption, but the bypass trust avoids a second tax on it when Clara dies.

Could Elmont use the bypass trust device to save the second tax if Clara were his daughter rather than his sister? Yes, but only on the first $250,000 in the trust. Any amount over that would be taxable as if it were part of Clara's estate, because of the generation-skipping rule (see Chapter 2). But a trust paying income to a spouse, sister, or anyone else in your generation won't be taxed again when that beneficiary dies, even if the principal then goes to a child or grandchild.

Remember, a bypass trust doesn't save taxes on *your* estate. The purpose is to prevent the trust principal from being taxed when your immediate beneficiary dies. Suppose that beneficiary is a married son; he and his wife can leave their heirs $1.2 million tax-free. So if the money you bequeath them won't put their estate over the top, you don't need a bypass trust.

On the other hand, if your son is prosperous and doesn't need your money, you can leave it in trust for your grandchildren and make them the income beneficiaries as well. If you do that, the trust won't come under the generation-skipping rule, so there'll be no possibility of a second estate tax at your son's death. Furthermore, the income tax on the trust's earnings will probably be much less than if they went to your son.

What if you can't foresee whether your son will need the income or how big an estate he'll pile up? Then consider splitting your bequest between him and the grandchildren. For example, if you want him to have $300,000, leave $150,000 in the grandchildren's trust with income to your son. It's unlikely that the trust will grow to more than $250,000 by the time he dies, so there won't be a generation-skipping tax. Your will should provide that, in the event your son doesn't need his $150,000 share, he can disclaim it in favor of the grandchildren. That will keep it from being taxed in his estate.

EASE THE COST BURDEN ON YOUR HEIRS

It's not only taxes that shrink an estate. Executor's and attorney's fees can also take a sizable bite. A married doctor may possibly save some of that by naming his spouse as executor, but it's often hard for a single doctor to find a reliable person who will serve without pay. Naming a lawyer as executor could also reduce or eliminate one fee, but many lawyers might refuse to serve or be unsuitable. One solution is to consider a lifetime trust to reduce the value of the assets passing through probate (see Chapter 4).

Despite all efforts to trim them, taxes and administrative costs may still make heavy demands on a single doctor's estate. Unlike married colleagues, he or she can't use the unlimited marital deduction to stave off the tax blow until the surviving spouse dies. Life insurance is an effective means of dealing with this threat, especially if you keep the policy proceeds out of the taxable estate by transferring ownership to the beneficiary (see Chapter 5).

LIMIT THE DAMAGE OF DIVORCE

Divorce is bound to jolt any estate plan you may have drawn up during the marriage. Your will almost surely will have to be revised, even if the law in your state automatically revokes bequests to a divorced spouse. Very likely, the divorce settlement gives your ex-spouse a substantial portion of your income and assets, so you'll have to adjust the amounts earmarked to provide for your children and other dependents. Regardless of who has custody of your minor children, you'll probably want to leave their inheritance in trust until they come of age or perhaps longer. You'll need to decide how much discretion to allow the trustee in distributing the funds, and whether to give your former spouse a voice in the matter.

Forethought to the tax consequences of the divorce settlement can help relieve some of the financial pain. Listed here are the main areas where income and gift/estate tax problems are likely to arise, along with suggestions on how to handle them the best way for both spouses.

Support payments

In general, support payments are either tax-deductible by the payer and taxable as income to the recipient, or else nondeductible by the payer and tax-free to the recipient. Though gender makes no difference to the tax collector, let's equate payer with husband and recipient with wife, for ease of reference.

Since the husband is usually in a higher tax bracket than the wife, a support agreement that takes this into account can benefit both of them. Say the wife is asking a minimum of $20,000 a year tax-free. That would cost the husband $20,000 in after-tax dollars because he couldn't deduct any of it. Suppose he offered the wife $28,000 on condition that she pay the taxes. If she had little or no other income, she might net upwards of $23,000 after taxes instead of $20,000. At the same time, the husband's tax saving (42 percent or so) on the $28,000 payment might reduce his after-tax cost to less than $17,000 instead of $20,000. So each would be some $3,000 better off.

Note, however, that the divorce agreement can't arbitrarily declare the support payments to be tax-deductible by the husband. To have that status, they must comply with requirements laid down in the tax laws and regulations.

Any part of the payment earmarked for child support is not deductible. But if the agreement doesn't specify an amount for the child, the entire payment is considered to be alimony—not child support—for tax purposes, even though the ex-wife has custody of the child.

To be deductible, the alimony payment must be required by court decree or legal separation agreement and must end at the ex-wife's death or sooner. Also, if the annual total is more than $10,000, the payments must continue for at least six years, unless the ex-wife dies earlier or remarries. If the six-year rule isn't met, the husband loses part of the deduction. For example, if a $90,000 settlement is payable in six annual $15,000 installments, all of those payments will be deductible as alimony by the ex-husband, but if the money is to be paid out in five $18,000 installments, only $10,000 each year will be allowed as a deduction.

The installments can be unequal, but don't agree to make very large payments early on—for example, $30,000 in years one and two, and $7,500 in years three through six. Because the law has a built-in bias against such front-loading, you'd lose $25,000 in tax deductions.

Don't try to tie a future reduction in alimony to an event involving a child in your ex-spouse's custody. Suppose you agree to pay your spouse alimony of $2,500 a month currently, but only $2,000 after your child reaches a specified age, graduates from college, gets married, or whatever. The law holds that the $500-a-month difference is really disguised child support, so only $2,000 of your present $2,500 payment will be deductible on your income tax return.

This principle might apply even if the agreement merely called for a $500 monthly alimony reduction at a set time without mentioning the child. Say the lower payments are slated to start in 1995, and your child will turn 21 that year. That "coincidence" could cause the $500 to be treated as child support now.

It's worth re-emphasizing that any payment *not* required by a decree or separation agreement can't be deducted as alimony. For instance, you may be willing to pay your ex-wife's future medical expenses. If the agreement doesn't commit you to doing so, you can't claim any deduction for them. If it does, you deduct them in full as alimony. That makes them taxable income to your ex-spouse, but she may be able to claim an offsetting medical expense if she itemizes her deductions.

By the same token, any payment you make before the decree or agreement is effective can't be treated as alimony. That goes for any payment you make after your divorced spouse's death, even if it's required by the agreement. Suppose you've agreed to give your spouse $25,000 annually for 10 years—$20,000 as support plus $5,000 for relinquishing some property rights. You can tax-deduct the entire $25,000 as alimony if all payments are to end in case you ex dies sooner. But if you're obliged to continue paying $5,000 a year to your spouse's estate until the 10 years are up, only the $20,000 support payments count as alimony.

Property settlements

If you transfer assets to your ex-spouse, you need to consider the tax effect. Suppose you're obligated to pay her $75,000 under a court decree or a written agreement made in connection with the divorce. Instead of cash, you give her $75,000 worth of stock that originally cost you $50,000. You won't be taxed on the capital gain, but her cost basis will be $50,000—not the stock's current value—so she'll have a taxable gain when she sells. In reality, then, she'll be getting less than the amount due her. On the other hand, if the stock cost you more than the $75,000 it's worth now, she can claim a tax loss by selling it.

You generally won't have to pay gift tax on assets transferred under a divorce settlement, even though you're no longer husband and wife. Also, if your agreement calls for a transfer after your death, that will be considered a deductible estate expense, and therefore not subject to estate tax.

However, watch out for gift tax traps on post-divorce property transfers to your ex-spouse that *aren't* covered by the prior agreement. Let's say the divorce decree provides for joint ownership of your house, but you later voluntarily put title in your ex-spouse's name alone. You've made a gift of half the current value. You can claim the $10,000 annual gift tax exclusion, but the rest will be taxable to you. Had you transferred title while still married, you'd have avoided any gift tax.

Likewise be careful when you turn over property after your divorce in exchange for release from future support payments. If the property is worth more than the commuted value of the payments, the difference may be taxable as a gift.

Life insurance

You may agree to insure your life to protect your divorced spouse and children. If you want to tax-deduct the premiums, you must irrevocably assign absolute ownership and control of the policy to your ex-spouse, she must be the primary beneficiary, and the insurance must be the cash-value type, not term. If those three conditions are met, the premiums are alimony deductible by you and taxable income to her.

Even though the decree or agreement relieves you of any obligation to pay premiums if your spouse dies or remarries, it must *not* provide that ownership and control of the policy come back to you in those or any other circumstances. If your spouse collects on the policy, the proceeds are tax-free.

Trusts and annuities

A spouse's alimony can also be protected by transferring income-producing property to a trust or buying an annuity for her. Although you can't deduct the trust or annuity payments to your spouse on your tax return, the income is taxable to *her,* not to you. If a part of the payment represents return of capital—as it would in the case of an annuity—that portion is tax-free.

Even when there's no tax advantage to an alimony trust or annuity, it does increase the security of the payments. If your obligation to pay alimony ceases, any remaining trust principal may revert to you.

Housing expenses

If you agree to pay the mortgage, taxes, and insurance on a home owned by your divorced spouse, those outlays are tax-deductible as alimony. She must include them in her income but can claim itemized deductions for the mortgage interest and property taxes.

If *you* own the house and let your spouse live there rent-free, you get no alimony deduction for its rental value, though you can deduct the interest and taxes as with any other property. If the house is jointly owned, the deductions are allocated accordingly. Regardless of ownership, utility expenses you pay for your divorced spouse are treated as alimony.

Dependency exemptions

The general rule is that the parent who has custody of a child for all or the greater part of the year gets the exemption. But a written agreement with your spouse can give you the exemption even if you don't have custody. You must file a copy of the agreement with your annual return.

No matter who gets the exemption, if you pay any of your child's medical expenses, you can include those amounts in figuring your medical deduction, and the child-care credit can be claimed by the custodial parent if eligible. This credit is available to single parents who have to pay for the care of children under 15 in order to go to work.

How to choose and use advisers

To make sure that your estate plan will withstand any legal test it may be subjected to, the services of an attorney are absolutely indispensable. How to locate one who's suitable for you—and equally important, how to work with your counsel effectively and economically—is discussed below. However, even the most astute and capable lawyer can't be counted on to have expertise in all the diverse fields that bear upon your estate plan. From time to time, you'll find it desirable to call in specialists for advice on elements of the plan itself, as well as on its financial underpinnings. In addition to your attorney, those advisers might include consultants on insurance, investments, taxes, and practice management.

ESTATE-PLANNING ATTORNEY

Many general-practice lawyers have a number of standard wills on file, and if you go to one of them, you may well get such an off-the-shelf document without scrutiny of your particular financial and tax situation. A doctor's will should always be prepared as part of a comprehensive estate plan by an attorney who specializes in that field.

A good estate-planning attorney can also act as a traffic director for the other professionals you use—the accountant who gives you income tax assistance, the lawyer who handles your professional corporation and its retirement plan, your investment and business advisers, and so forth. The estate specialist can make sure that these advisers' efforts don't conflict.

Where to look for a lawyer

How do you find the attorney you need? Obviously, you must ask for recommendations. Here's a list of sources—and some drawbacks you should be sure to watch out for:

Your colleagues have many of the same interests as you have, and they are likely to have similar legal problems, too. However, in accepting a recommendation, make sure it's based on solid results achieved by the lawyer, not just a friendly association. Check with friends and relatives, too, but again get them to supply concrete evidence of satisfactory performance.

Your accountant is undoubtedly knowledgeable about lawyers in your locality and should be well enough informed of your circumstances to suggest a suitable candidate. Bank officials, insurance agents, and stockbrokers also have frequent contacts with lawyers, but in highly specialized ways. More often than not, their opinions will be colored by the amount of business an attorney pushes their way. Accept their recommendations only if you know them well and respect their judgment.

Lawyer referral services are seldom very helpful. They mainly list attorneys who are hard up for clients, new in town, or fresh out of school.

Check the credentials

No matter where you get your recommendations, you can check them out in the *Martindale-Hubbell Law Directory*. It lists all licensed attorneys in the country, gives their ages, degrees, and professional associations, and reveals how other attorneys rate their abilities. The directory is available at courts, bar association offices, and university or public libraries.

Talk about fees

Don't be shy about asking how much a lawyer will charge. Many bill on an hourly basis because time spent may vary widely from client to client even for the same procedure. Hourly billing for the administration of an estate may often be fairer than charging a percentage of the assets involved, an estate attorney points out:

"Suppose a person dies leaving an estate of $1 million in publicly traded stocks and bonds that can be easily transferred and readily valued for tax purposes. Let's also assume that there is an amicable family situation and that the will was properly drafted. Charging on a percentage basis might result in a fee of $25,000, and that could be grossly inequitable for the heirs.

"On the other hand, suppose a person left a $100,000 apartment building encumbered with mortgages and liens. Suppose further that the will is ambiguous and that there are two women claiming they were married to the decedent at the time of his death. In that case, the fee set at the same percentage might come to $2,500—an amount that would be unfair to the attorney. To avoid such situations, our firm bills for estate work largely on the basis of time spent.'' (State law may control the fee, however; see Chapter 4.)

Many lawyers used to draw up wills and trusts at bargain rates in the hope of being rewarded by fees for handling the settlement of the estate later on. But if the client moved away or the executor chose another lawyer, the one who drew up the documents was out of luck. This hit-or-miss method has fallen out of favor among lawyers. Now most charge more realistic fees for the paperwork, plus additional amounts for consultations.

To hold down your costs, make sure you're prepared with the information your lawyer will need when you confer with him. If you're going to discuss your estate, take along a list of all the assets you and your spouse own. You may also have to know details about your life insurance and your retirement plan. Ask your lawyer beforehand what information he'll require and what key decisions you and your spouse will have to make. (See Box 12A.)

In dealing with some legal matters, you may be better off bringing other advisers along when you see your attorney. For instance, a planning session involving the disposition of business interests often goes best when the tax adviser is present.

Consider calling on less highly paid consultants to help with the preliminaries. For example, your management consultant might prepare an outline of the options to consider in a buy-and-sell agreement or an employment contract. You'd then take the outline to the conference with the attorney, who would discuss the matter with you and draft the legal document. That way he'd spend less time than if he were starting from scratch.

Remember, when you see your lawyer the meter is running. Try to organize your thoughts and your questions so that you get all of the relevant material into the discussion. If you come up with a significant fact after you leave, the lawyer may have to redo some of the work, and you may wind up paying extra charges.

LIFE INSURANCE AGENT

An insurance program designed by a poor agent can turn out to be a costly mistake for you and your family. Answers you obtain to the following questions may help you decide which agent should get your business:

☐ *Can the agent offer more than one company's policies?* Life insurance salespeople come in four varieties. The best group to choose are the *brokerage agents,* sometimes called *independent agents.* They're set up to do business with any insurer. They'll have their favorites, but their obligation is to get you the best benefits at the cheapest price. Because they aren't dependent upon any one company for their livelihood, they should at least be able to come up with bids from several competing companies.

BOX 12A
What to do before you see your lawyer

You can save time and money if you dig out the details concerning the disposition of your estate and discuss key decisions with your spouse before you see your lawyer. Here's a handy checklist:

Papers to get

☐ Inventory or net-worth statement
☐ Last income tax return and all gift tax returns
☐ Deeds to real estate
☐ Life insurance and annuity policies
☐ Keogh and other retirement-plan statements and plan documents
☐ Partnership and stockholders' agreements and relevant financial statements
☐ Divorce or separation papers
☐ Copies of present wills
☐ Estimates of possible inheritances from others
☐ Copies of trust documents if you, your spouse, or your children are beneficiaries

Decisions to consider

☐ Should money be left to your spouse in trust?
☐ Should the special needs of a child be taken care of by a larger share?
☐ What relatives, other persons, and charities do you want to benefit?
(List names and amounts.)
☐ Whom do you want as guardians, executors, and trustees?
(List names.)
☐ When do you want your children to receive their shares?

By contrast, *career agents* are under contract to sell one company's policies exclusively. The only time they can officially sidestep that limitation is when their primary carrier doesn't have a suitable type of coverage for you or won't take on your risk. Unless you're sure you want to deal with this agent's company, you'll do better to go with the independent agent.

The other two types of life insurance agents are to be avoided. One, the *direct writers,* work on a salaried basis for one insurer only and can't shop around for you at all. The final type are *general brokers*—not to be confused with the brokerage agents mentioned above. The general brokers sell property and liability insurance primarily. They've also passed the life insurance licensing exam. However, it's virtually impossible for any agent to have enough expertise and knowledge in every field of insurance to do the best job for you.

☐ *What are the agent's experience and background?* Five years in the business is a reasonable minimum to set. Any agent you use should have qualified as a Chartered Life Underwriter. That doesn't guarantee competence, but at least it shows he's passed an exam based on an extensive training program that concentrates on insurance and also includes a smattering of financial-planning courses.

How to choose and use advisers

☐ *Does the agent try to sell you the wrong kind of insurance?* Unfortunately, the policies many agents push aren't what you'd buy if you knew what they know. Whole-life insurance—the kind that accumulates cash value—may have a place in many doctors' portfolios as a savings vehicle. But it's not appropriate for all.

One reason many insurance agents favor and recommend whole life is that they often earn far more in commissions than for selling a less-expensive term policy. Your agent should at least be willing to discuss the merits and drawbacks of different coverages and be able to back any recommendations with cost comparisons.

There are two ways to measure the real cost of a whole-life policy: One, called net cost, is the total you'll pay in premiums over, say, 20 years' time minus your estimated dividends and the cash surrender value at the end of that period. The other, known as the interest-adjusted cost, allows for the interest you lose by using your money to pay premiums instead of investing it elsewhere. The interest-adjusted method is widely recognized as the more realistic way to compare policy costs.

If you want to check the differences in the true cost of policies an agent is touting, you can look the figures up in *Flitcraft Compend*, which is available in most public libraries. That book, published annually by A. M. Best Company, lists interest-adjusted cost comparisons for most policies you'll be offered. Salespeople who bring it along or suggest that you consult it have a point in their favor.

☐ *How much time is the agent willing to spend?* It should be enough time to make a thorough-going analysis of your situation and develop an overall program that meets your objectives. The agent should be able to justify any policies recommended on the basis of what you earn now and project for the future, your obligations, and your other investments. After you buy, the agent should be in touch at least once a year to see if changes are needed.

Don't be unduly impressed if the agent offers a computer analysis of your insurance needs. All this may amount to is saving time by getting a few facts from you, feeding them into the computer, and presenting what purports to be an "individualized plan." It might omit important details concerning your assets, liabilities, and personal wishes that should have been elicited from you. Computer analysis is often a cloak for an agent to hide laziness or lack of expertise.

INVESTMENT COUNSELOR

An ethical investment counselor is comparable to a lawyer in the way he works. His advice is direct, personal, unbiased, and confidential. He has nothing to sell; he takes no commissions. You pay him the same fee no matter what securities you buy or sell.

What you get

What does he do for his fee? After he has studied your entire financial situation (your assets, income, insurance, dependents, retirement plans, etc.), he suggests a long-range program to meet your objectives. And he tells you specifically which securities should be bought and sold to launch that program. If you want, he will merely give you his recommendations, and you can place the buy and sell orders with your broker personally. Or you can give him authority to place the orders for you.

Either way, the counselor usually doesn't hold your securities, and he gets no share of the brokerage fees. You can retain full control over your account, or you can delegate it. You're perfectly free, whenever you wish, to modify your arrangement with him or to drop it entirely.

Once every three or six months, he'll send you a detailed accounting of your holdings and of any action that has been taken on them. During the intervening period, he will continually monitor the securities you hold and study possible replacements for them. If he believes a holding is turning sour, he'll notify you immediately and recommend a switch.

A good investment counselor will also keep an eye on your tax liability, to make sure transactions are timed for the biggest tax advantage. Naturally, the bracket you're in will strongly influence his choice of securities for you.

Broker vs. counselor

A good broker stands ready to tell you which stocks to buy or sell and when. Is he likely to be a better source of advice than an investment counselor?

An investment counselor gets paid for one thing only—his advice on the management of your portfolio. Although some large brokerage firms charge for research services, a broker's income comes mostly from commissions, and their size depends on the volume and frequency of the buy and sell transactions you make. Due to his interest in how often you buy and sell, the broker may be biased against investing for the long term. Taken to extremes, this can lead to the churning of your account—to transactions made primarily for the purpose of generating commissions for the broker, not for sound investment reasons.

For a certain kind of investor, though, a broker is a better choice than an investment counselor. If you're a doctor inclined to be a trader who goes in and out of stocks to pick up a few points here and there, regardless of how short a time you've held a stock or what its long-term potential is, a broker with a day-to-day feeling for the market can do a better job than a counselor.

Fees

An investment counselor's fee nearly always depends on the amount of money you have to invest. There are generally two ways he'll settle on a fee—a minimum flat fee or a percentage rate. For handling a large portfolio, it's fairly common practice to charge 0.5 percent, or $5 per $1,000 worth of assets. Fees range upward to 1 or 2 percent for smaller portfolios.

For a small investor, the cost of hiring an investment counselor may be too high. That's because the annual minimum most counselors charge is on the order of $500, and sometimes it's more. The less money you invest, then, the relatively more expensive it becomes to acquire personal investment guidance.

Since investment counseling firms charge a percentage of the value of your portfolio, they may place a minimum on the size of portfolio they'll accept. While most of their clients have upwards of $100,000 to invest, some counselors work with investors who have only $20,000 to $30,000. And a few of them will handle even smaller accounts.

"We're much more interested in the potential for growth of a doctor's account than in its initial size," says the head of one counseling firm. He does not add—but it's an obvious fact—that the amount of attention a $20,000 account gets (or needs) will be far less than that given to a $200,000 account.

How to choose a counselor

If you decide to use an investment counselor, you might choose one who belongs to the Investment Counsel Association of America. The ICAA sets high standards of integrity and professionalism for its member counseling firms, and awards a Chartered Investment Counselor certificate to individuals in those firms who have at least five years' experience and pass a stringent examination. (For a list of its 100 or so member firms, contact the ICAA, 50 Broad Street, New York, NY 10004 (phone 212-344-0999).

However, many firms that aren't members do a creditable job of research, securities analysis, and counseling. The problem is to find out which are good. Merely being registered with the Securities and Exchange Commission means little. *All* counselors must register if they solicit clients outside their home state, and almost anyone can qualify so long as he hasn't been convicted of fraud.

One way to judge a counselor, apart from membership in the ICAA or recommendations from friends, associates, or your bank, is by your own personal reaction to him. It's certainly not an infallible test, but it's a beginning. If you're unable to arrange a face-to-face meeting with him, at least make it a point to talk to him on the telephone.

After you've had a positive reaction to a counselor, ask him about his organization. What kind of setup does he have for researching economic conditions and market trends? How adequate is his staff of securities analysts? Do these people have advanced degrees in business administration or economics? Are they entitled to put "CFA," for Chartered Financial Analyst after their names? To earn this designation, they must have passed rigorous exams in securities analysis and economics.

Performance

All the research in the world will mean nothing, however, unless an investment counselor can use it to construct a portfolio that will give you the kind of performance you want. If you ask what sort of results he's been getting for his present clients, he may tell you that he can't reveal clients' names and their portfolios' performance, as a matter of protecting their privacy. Or he may tell you that SEC regulations limit his freedom to show you his track record. Still another reason for reluctance, often unstated, is that counselors generally prefer not to think of themselves as being in a performance horse race. However, a counselor should at least be willing to show you the long-term results of a group of anonymous accounts similar to yours. (The ICAA recommends a performance-report format for its members to follow.)

Some investment counselors run their own mutual funds as showcase operations, and it's reasonable to judge what kind of performance a counselor can get for his private clients from what he gets for his public operation.

What kind of performance *should* you expect from a counselor? At least that your portfolio will do better than the market averages and also outpace the rate of inflation.

Even the most capable counselor may make mistakes with your money. "Counselors don't claim to be infallible or omniscient," says one. "A doctor could collect the same facts. But compiling, interpreting, and applying those facts takes time, training, and experience. Investment counselors are specialists in that work. Their fee might be the best investment you ever make." By the same token, the fee might be a needless expense if you have the time, ability, and temperament to handle investments on your own.

TAX CONSULTANT

A tax consultant must know not only the tax business but the doctor business as well. So your colleagues are a logical source of recommendations. Does your tax adviser have to be an accountant? No, but it helps. In most areas, you have a choice of two kinds: CPAs or noncertified accountants. The CPAs are at the top of the accounting ladder. They've passed a stiff exam, most likely are college graduates, and are subject to professional discipline and a code of ethics. But they may not be as suitable as a noncertified accountant who has specialized in doctors' tax problems.

What about a lawyer? Possibly—but make sure the attorney has a knowledge of accounting. And don't get stuck with a high-priced pro whose principal occupation is tax work for large corporations.

Though the IRS won't prescribe where you can go for tax help, it's choosy about whom it will allow to represent you at its proceedings. Lawyers and CPAs are automatically eligible, but uncertified accountants and other tax advisers can be enrolled to practice before the IRS only by passing a tough written test.

If your present adviser isn't a lawyer, CPA, or "enrolled agent," that in itself is no reason to fire him. If he prepares your return, the IRS will let him represent you, up to a point. You can have your preparer with you at an audit. He can also take your place at the audit, but can speak only with regard to a return he prepared himself. And he can't appear before or correspond in your name with the higher echelons in the IRS structure.

Whatever your favored candidate's professional qualifications, find out for sure whether he'll be available when you need him. As a rule, you'll have an easier time with a person who's based close to home. If you hire someone in a large city many miles away, you might end up seeing only his junior assistant. Also, you can run up large telephone bills. But don't sacrifice quality for the sake of proximity.

CPA fees commonly range from $50 to $100 or more per hour, depending on the section of the country. Whether you pay your tax consultant a flat fee or by the hour, get a commitment as to what work he'll do for you. That could include making financial analyses for you, as well as checking your books periodically and making out your tax returns.

Most consultants feel it's desirable to examine a physician's records regularly throughout the year, not just at tax time. How often? Four times a year seems to be the consensus, but monthly visits might be appropriate for a very busy practice. Periodic checks make it easier for your consultant to keep your records in shape to withstand IRS audits and to spot developing financial problems. A side benefit of having your books reviewed at regular intervals is the possibility of nipping embezzlement in the bud.

Though you shouldn't expect your tax adviser to give you stock tips, you'd do well to ask his opinion on tax shelters you're considering, along with other investments that could affect your tax picture seriously. His eye for figures can also help you evaluate the pros and cons of business or real estate deals you may be contemplating.

PRACTICE MANAGEMENT CONSULTANT

Accountants who have a number of physicians as clients can often serve as practice management consultants. Normally your accountant is already familiar with your retirement plan and tax situation, partnership or corporate relations, office operations and expenses, and billing and collection procedures. If he knows how his other doctor clients handle these matters, he can usually provide competent advice without requiring a lot of time to orient himself. By employing him in this capacity, you avoid the expenditure of time and money involved in establishing a totally new professional relationship.

Estate planning strategies for physicians

However, while accountants may be well qualified in some aspects of your practice, management consultants generally have more expertise when it comes to such things as personnel policies, fee structures, patient relations, appointment scheduling, and office site selection and layout. A management consultant's advice may be particularly useful if you're buying, selling, or reorganizing a practice.

The number of practice management firms in the US is estimated at more than 500, with at least one in every state. Many consultants provide full service only in one or several neighboring states, but will go elsewhere for one-shot consultations if the client pays expenses.

If you aren't able to obtain suitable recommendations from other doctors or dentists, you can get names and addresses of reliable consultants in your area by writing to the Society of Professional Business Consultants, 221 North LaSalle Street, Chicago, IL 60601 (phone 312-346-1600), or to the Society of Medical-Dental Management Consultants, 4959 Olson Memorial Highway, Minneapolis, MN 55422 (phone 612-544-9621).

The Institute of Certified Professional Business Consultants administers examinations and confers the title "Certified Professional Business Consultant" (CPBC) on those who pass a two-part exam (half practice management and half financial management). In order to qualify, candidates must have limited their work to professional management consulting for at least five years and must subscribe to the institute's code of ethics and rules of professional conduct.

Management consultants operate in different ways. Some make monthly visits, during which they check your financial records, review collections and unpaid accounts, advise you on business methods and office equipment, and confer with you on other practice matters. Other consultants visit only quarterly or annually. Some specialize in practice-building or collection techniques, or prefer to work with medical groups or corporations.

So before you engage a consultant, make sure he's interested and equipped to tackle the kinds of problems you're facing. Ask him for a list of doctors using his services. Find out about his firm's research facilities and the availability of data on other practices against which to measure your own.

Most consultants charge $50 to $100 an hour. The rate applies not only to time spent in your office, but also to travel time and time spent writing reports for you. Daily rates, among the minority who bill that way, range from $250 to $1,000. Firms that handle all office bookkeeping and billing may base their fees on practice volume; one leading firm charges its full-service clients a minimum of $350 a month.

As with most things, there are no bargains in management consulting services. If you're quoted fees much lower than those cited above, the consultant may be underqualified, or may be planning to load you up with insurance or other items on which he'll collect commissions. Ethical consultants pledge not to take such commissions.

AVOIDING BAD ADVICE

There will be times when your advisers should work as a team, with management consultant, accountant, insurance agent, and attorney each contributing special expertise. For instance, all of them should get into the act when you incorporate and set up a fringe-benefit package and retirement plan for yourself and your employees. Estate planning and income tax problems will often call for joint input, and so will a major investment like the purchase of your own medical building.

Inevitably, some disagreements will come up. When they do, you'll have to listen to all sides of the argument, ask yourself who's really most objective and knowledgeable in the area under discussion, and then make your own decision—or seek additional competent advice.

Don't hesitate to switch advisers when you're dissatisfied. If you're dubious about any of them, ask the others about him. Most will give you a forthright opinion.

Don't put too much reliance on the fact that a consultant is licensed by the state. Licensing may only indicate that he has paid a fee. In some fields, professionals aren't required to show evidence of competence or integrity before being granted a license.

People who sell investments go by different titles—stockbrokers, registered representatives, account executives—and most are licensed. But make no mistake about it: They're salespeople, not consultants. Now and then you'll encounter one who takes the long view and puts clients' interests first. But many investment salespeople are concerned only with closing the immediate transaction.

Most advisers who call themselves financial planners are really insurance salespeople. The fact that such advisers will take a commission on an insurance sale doesn't necessarily mean that they aren't expert at what they do, or that they place their own financial interest ahead of their clients'. But they should be willing to disclose their income sources, and be able to convince you of their objectivity.

APPENDIX 1

Will-review checklist

Changes in your family or financial circumstances may furnish good reasons to alter your will, so you should review it periodically. (See sample will in Appendix 6.) This checklist will help you pinpoint weak spots that call for revision:

☐ *Have your jointly owned assets increased in value?* Since these pass automatically to your spouse or other co-owner at your death, a big jump in their worth could disrupt your estate plan. If you contemplate shifting ownership as a remedy, you'll need guidance from a competent adviser to prevent adverse income or estate tax consequences.

☐ *Has an heir or insurance beneficiary died?* If it's an heir, don't assume the bequest is void or passes to *his* heir automatically. Unless your will expressly says who gets the bequest, it may go to someone you wouldn't want to have it. If an insurance beneficiary has died, the proceeds of the policy could become part of your estate, increasing administrative costs and taxes. And if a minor such as a grandchild or niece becomes the beneficiary because her parent has died, this could entail complicated court proceedings, involving avoidable expense and inconvenience.

☐ *Is your executor or trustee still able to serve?* If your brother, lawyer, friend, or whoever you designated has moved away, been disabled, or become too old to act effectively, make a change now. If you don't, a court may wind up appointing someone you wouldn't consider desirable—at a higher cost than may be necessary. If you have individuals as trustees of any long-lasting trusts, it's usually best to name a bank or other institution as the ultimate successor trustee to assure that there will always be one.

☐ *Do you have a new child?* In a few states, the birth of a child may revoke a will completely. In most others, the will stands, and the child automatically receives a share of the estate. (Adoption usually has the same effect as natural birth.) What the state law decrees may not be what you had in mind, however.

☐ *Are your children's guardians still suitable?* A number of years ago you may have named a married couple as the guardians of your children. If they've since divorced or moved or one has died, a change may be needed.

147

☐ *Has your marital status changed?* In some states, marriage automatically revokes an existing will. So a new will must be drawn up, or else the law will determine how the estate is divided. If you were divorced after you made your will, you'll want to revise it even if your former spouse's bequest is automatically revoked. Otherwise, that part of your estate may not go where you now intend. If you have children from an earlier marriage, a change in your will to conform to the revised federal tax law may be especially desirable. A trust for your children can now qualify for the marital deduction, provided your spouse gets all the trust income during her lifetime.

☐ *Have you moved to or acquired property in a different state?* The laws of your new state might drastically alter or even invalidate some provisions of your will. Your executor may no longer be convenient or eligible. Complications can be particularly severe if you've moved to a community-property state from one that isn't; property rights of husbands and wives may be inconsistent with the provisions of a will written in a non-community-property state. Even if your present will remains valid, you should probably sign it and have it witnessed again to spare your estate the expense and time required to get depositions from out-of-state witnesses.

☐ *Are the provisions regarding your retirement plan outmoded?* Unless your spouse is the sole beneficiary, all of your plan funds will be part of your taxable estate, thanks to recent changes in the law. Even if that's no problem, growth or modification of the plan may call for revisions in your will.

APPENDIX 2

State death taxes

There are two types: an estate tax, which is a liability on the estate and is based on its size, usually after an overall exemption and permissible deductions; and an inheritance tax, which is a liability on each heir and is generally based on the size of the legacy above a specified exempt amount. Only Nevada imposes no death taxes at all. A score of states impose only an estate tax equal to the "state tax paid" credit that can be claimed against the federal estate tax (see Box 2F); if there's no federal tax payable on the estate, no state tax is due either. The remaining states impose either an inheritance or estate tax; if that's less than the credit allowable against the federal tax, the state gets the difference by collecting a supplementary estate tax.

Life insurance proceeds are often tax exempt unless paid to the estate (rather than to a named individual or trust beneficiary) or unless the proceeds are required to be used to pay taxes or debts of the estate. However, many states follow federal law and tax the insurance proceeds if the decedent owned the policy.

State	Type of tax	Spouse's exemption	Child's exemption	Insurance taxed if owned by decedent
Alabama	Estate (federal credit only)	NA	NA	Yes
Alaska	Estate (federal credit only)	NA	NA	Yes
Arizona	Estate (federal credit only)	NA	NA	Yes
Arkansas	Estate (federal credit only)	NA	NA	Yes
California	Estate (federal credit only)	NA	NA	Yes
Colorado	Estate (federal credit only)	NA	NA	Yes
Connecticut	Inheritance	$100,000	$20,000	No[1]
Delaware	Inheritance	$ 70,000	$ 3,000	No

[1] All proceeds are exempt.

State	Type of tax	Spouse's exemption	Child's exemption	Insurance taxed if owned by decedent
District of Columbia	Inheritance	$ 5,000	$ 5,000	No
Florida	Estate (federal credit only)	NA	NA	Yes
Georgia	Estate (federal credit only)	NA	NA	Yes
Hawaii	Estate (federal credit only)	NA	NA	Yes
Idaho	Inheritance	All	$50,000[2]	No
Illinois	Estate (federal credit only)	NA	NA	Yes
Indiana	Inheritance	All	$10,000[3]	No
Iowa	Inheritance	$180,000[4]	$50,000	No
Kansas	Inheritance	All	$30,000	No
Kentucky	Inheritance	$50,000	$20,000[5]	No
Louisiana	Inheritance	$20,000[6,7]	$20,000	No
Maine	Estate (federal credit only)[7]	NA	NA	Yes
Maryland	Inheritance	None[8]	None[8]	No
Massachusetts	Estate	NA	NA	Yes
Michigan	Inheritance	All	$10,000	No
Minnesota	Estate	NA[9]	NA[9]	Yes
Mississippi	Estate	NA[10]	NA[10]	Yes[11]
Missouri	Estate (federal credit only)	NA	NA	Yes
Montana	Inheritance	All	All	Yes[12]
Nebraska	Inheritance	All	$10,000	No
Nevada	No death tax	—	—	—
New Hampshire	Inheritance	All	All	No
New Jersey	Inheritance	$15,000	$15,000	No

[2]If minor; otherwise, $30,000.
[3]If minor; otherwise, $5,000.
[4]All exempt if death occurs after 1987.
[5]If infant; otherwise, $5,000.
[6]Of decedent's separate property; spouse's share of community property is exempt.
[7]Inheritance tax is repealed effective July 1, 1986.
[8]Taxed at 1 percent; all others, 10 percent.
[9]All of spouse's share is covered by the marital deduction; a $600,000 exemption applies to the balance of the estate (effective after 1986).
[10]A $175,625 exemption applies to the entire estate.
[11]First $20,000 is not taxed if payable to a named beneficiary.
[12]However owned, all proceeds are taxable except the first $50,000.

State	Type of tax	Spouse's exemption	Child's exemption	Insurance taxed if owned by decedent
New Mexico	Estate (federal credit only)	NA	NA	Yes
New York	Estate	NA[13]	NA[13]	Yes
North Carolina	Inheritance	None[14]	None[14]	Yes
North Dakota	Estate (federal credit only)	NA	NA	Yes
Ohio	Estate	NA[15]	NA	No
Oklahoma	Estate	NA[16]	NA[16]	Yes
Oregon	Estate (federal credit only)[17]	NA	NA	Yes
Pennsylvania	Inheritance	None[18]	None[18]	No[1]
Rhode Island	Estate	NA[19]	NA	Yes
South Carolina	Estate	NA[20]	NA[20]	Yes
South Dakota	Inheritance	All	$30,000	No
Tennessee	Inheritance	$100,000[21]	$100,000[21]	Yes
Texas	Estate (federal credit only)	NA	NA	Yes
Utah	Estate (federal credit only)	NA	NA	Yes
Vermont	Estate (federal credit only)	NA	NA	Yes
Virginia	Estate (federal credit only)	NA	NA	Yes
Washington	Estate (federal credit only)	NA	NA	Yes
West Virginia	Inheritance	$30,000	$10,000	No
Wisconsin	Inheritance	All	$50,000	Yes
Wyoming	Estate (federal credit only)	NA	NA	Yes

[13]A $50,000 exemption applies to the entire estate.
[14]A total tax credit of $4,650 applies.
[15]Marital deduction covers half the estate.
[16]All of spouse's share is covered by the marital deduction; a $175,000 total exemption applies to legacies for other relatives.
[17]Inheritance tax is repealed effective 1987.
[18]Taxed at 6 percent; all others, 15 percent.
[19]Marital deduction covers $175,000.
[20]A $120,000 exemption applies to the entire estate.
[21]Rises in stages to $600,000 after 1989.

Source: Commerce Clearing House.

APPENDIX 3

Present value of annuities

Use Table A to compute the present value if the term is the beneficiary's life. For example, your beneficiary is to receive a $20,000 lifelong annuity from your pension plan after your death. If the beneficiary is 53 at that time, the value of the annuity for estate tax purposes is 8.2028 times $20,000, or $164,056.

Suppose instead that the beneficiary is to get the annuity for a fixed term regardless of age. In that case, use Table B to figure the value. For instance, a $20,000 annuity payable for 10 years would be worth 6.1446 times $20,000, or $122,892.

TABLE A
Life annuity

Age of annuitant[1]	Multiplier[2]	Age of annuitant[1]	Multiplier[2]
0	9.7188	40	9.1571
1	9.8988	41	9.1030
2	9.9017	42	9.0457
3	9.9008	43	8.9855
4	9.8981	44	8.9221
5	9.8938	45	8.8558
6	9.8884	46	8.7863
7	9.8822	47	8.7137
8	9.8748	48	8.6374
9	9.8663	49	8.5578
10	9.8565	50	8.4743
11	9.8453	51	8.3874
12	9.8329	52	8.2969
13	9.8198	53	8.2028
14	9.8066	54	8.1054
15	9.7937	55	8.0046
16	9.7815	56	7.9006
17	9.7700	57	7.7931
18	9.7590	58	7.6822
19	9.7480	59	7.5675
20	9.7365	60	7.4491
21	9.7245	61	7.3267
22	9.7120	62	7.2002
23	9.6986	63	7.0696
24	9.6841	64	6.9352
25	9.6678	65	6.7970
26	9.6495	66	6.6551
27	9.6290	67	6.5098
28	9.6062	68	6.3610
29	9.5813	69	6.2086
30	9.5543	70	6.0522
31	9.5254	71	5.8914
32	9.4942	72	5.7261
33	9.4608	73	5.5571
34	9.4250	74	5.3862
35	9.3868		
36	9.3460		
37	9.3026		
38	9.2567		
39	9.2083		

[1]On birthday nearest to valuation date.
[2]Assumes an annual payment at end of year; for monthly payments, multiply factor shown by 1.045 and apply result to yearly total. If payments are at beginning of period, calculate as above and add one payment.

TABLE B
Fixed-term annuity

Number of years	Multiplier*	Number of years	Multiplier*
1	.9091	31	9.4790
2	1.7355	32	9.5264
3	2.4869	33	9.5694
4	3.1699	34	9.6086
5	3.7908	35	9.6442
6	4.3553	36	9.6765
7	4.8684	37	9.7059
8	5.3349	38	9.7327
9	5.7590	39	9.7570
10	6.1446	40	9.7791
11	6.4951	41	9.7991
12	6.8137	42	9.8174
13	7.1034	43	9.8340
14	7.3667	44	9.8491
15	7.6061	45	9.8628
16	7.8237	46	9.8753
17	8.0216	47	9.8866
18	8.2014	48	9.8969
19	8.3649	49	9.9063
20	8.5136	50	9.9148
21	8.6487	51	9.9226
22	8.7715	52	9.9296
23	8.8832	53	9.9360
24	8.9847	54	9.9418
25	9.0770	55	9.9471
26	9.1609	56	9.9519
27	9.2372	57	9.9563
28	9.3066	58	9.9603
29	9.3696	59	9.9639
30	9.4269	60	9.9672

*Assumes an annual payment at end of year; for monthly payments, multiply factor shown by 1.045 and apply result to yearly total. If payments are at beginning of period, multiply by 1.1 for annual payments or by 1.0534 for monthly payments.

Source: Internal Revenue Service.

APPENDIX 4

Present value of remainder interests

If you give away property but retain the income from it (or the use of it), the gift is worth less than the property's full value. The same is true if you give away the income but not the principal. Table A shows the value of the income interest if it's for life (a "life estate") and the value of the remainder; note that the two fractions add up to 1. Table B shows the values when the income interest is for a fixed term. For example, if you retain the income from a $50,000 property for 20 years, the value of the remainder is only 0.148644 times $50,000, or $7,432.

TABLE A
Life estate

Age of income recipient*	Value of income interest	Value of remainder interest	Age of income recipient*	Value of income interest	Value of remainder interest
0	.97188	.02812	40	.91571	.08429
1	.98988	.01012	41	.91030	.08970
2	.99017	.00983	42	.90457	.09543
3	.99008	.00992	43	.89855	.10145
4	.98981	.01019	44	.89221	.10779
5	.98938	.01062	45	.88558	.11442
6	.98884	.01116	46	.87863	.12137
7	.98822	.01178	47	.87137	.12863
8	.98748	.01252	48	.86374	.13626
9	.98663	.01337	49	.85578	.14422
10	.98565	.01435	50	.84743	.15257
11	.98453	.01547	51	.83874	.16126
12	.98329	.01671	52	.82969	.17031
13	.98198	.01802	53	.82028	.17972
14	.98066	.01934	54	.81054	.18946
15	.97937	.02063	55	.80046	.19954
16	.97815	.02185	56	.79006	.20994
17	.97700	.02300	57	.77931	.22069
18	.97590	.02410	58	.76822	.23178
19	.97480	.02520	59	.75675	.24325
20	.97365	.02635	60	.74491	.25509
21	.97245	.02755	61	.73267	.26733
22	.97120	.02880	62	.72002	.27998
23	.96986	.03014	63	.70696	.29304
24	.96814	.03159	64	.69352	.30648
25	.96678	.03322	65	.67970	.32030
26	.96495	.03505	66	.66551	.33449
27	.96290	.03710	67	.65098	.34902
28	.96062	.03938	68	.63610	.36390
29	.95813	.04187	69	.62086	.37914
30	.95543	.04457	70	.60522	.39478
31	.95254	.04746	71	.58914	.41086
32	.94942	.05058	72	.57261	.42739
33	.94608	.05392	73	.55571	.44429
34	.94250	.05750	74	.53862	.46138
35	.93868	.06132	75	.52149	.47851
36	.93460	.06540	76	.50441	.49559
37	.93026	.06974	77	.48742	.51258
38	.92567	.07433	78	.47049	.52951
39	.92083	.07917	79	.45357	.54643

*On birthday nearest to valuation date.

TABLE B
Fixed-term income interest

Number of years	Value of income interest	Value of remainder interest	Number of years	Value of income interest	Value of remainder interest
1	.090909	.909091	31	.947901	.052099
2	.173554	.826446	32	.952638	.047362
3	.248685	.751315	33	.956943	.043057
4	.316987	.683013	34	.960857	.039143
5	.379079	.620921	35	.964416	.035584
6	.435526	.564474	36	.967651	.032349
7	.486842	.513158	37	.970592	.029408
8	.533493	.466507	38	.973265	.026735
9	.575902	.424098	39	.975696	.024304
10	.614457	.385543	40	.977905	.022095
11	.649506	.350494	41	.979914	.020086
12	.681369	.318631	42	.981740	.018260
13	.710336	.289664	43	.983400	.016600
14	.736669	.263331	44	.984909	.015091
15	.760608	.239392	45	.986281	.013719
16	.782371	.217629	46	.987528	.012472
17	.802155	.197845	47	.988662	.011338
18	.820141	.179859	48	.989693	.010307
19	.836492	.163508	49	.990630	.009370
20	.851356	.148644	50	.991481	.008519
21	.864869	.135131	51	.992256	.007744
22	.877154	.122846	52	.992960	.007040
23	.888322	.111678	53	.993600	.006400
24	.898474	.101526	54	.994182	.005818
25	.907704	.092296	55	.994711	.005289
26	.916095	.083905	56	.995191	.004809
27	.923722	.076278	57	.995629	.004371
28	.930657	.069343	58	.996026	.003974
29	.936961	.063039	59	.996387	.003613
30	.942691	.057309	60	.996716	.003284

Source: Internal Revenue Service.

APPENDIX 5

Gift tax return

As explained in Chapter 10, gifts of more than $10,000 a year to an individual are normally taxable, but the tax-free limit is increased to $20,000 if your spouse consents to the gift. To take advantage of this "gift-splitting" rule, you must file a gift tax return, and your spouse must sign the consent statement printed on the form. A married couple can generally use the short gift tax form (709-A) unless one or both made other gifts that would be subject to tax even if split—e.g., a gift of a future interest, or gifts to one person totalling more than $20,000 during the year.* In that case, you must file the long form (709), which also allows for split gifts.

Schedule B of Form 709 calls for a recap of prior-year gift tax returns. That helps determine how much lifetime gift/estate tax credit you have left. Until all of the credit is used up, you don't actually pay anything, even on taxable gifts.

Notice that both 709 and 709-A ask you to list your adjusted basis (usually your cost) for each gift. If the recipient should sell the gift, he has to use your basis to figure the capital gain.

---

*You also can't use the short form for gifts of real estate.

Form **709-A**
(Rev. July 1982)
Department of the Treasury
Internal Revenue Service

United States Short Form Gift Tax Return
For gifts made after December 31, 1981
(For "Privacy Act" notice, see the Form 1040 instructions)
Calendar Year 19.............

OMB No. 1545–0021
Expires 6–30–85

Donor's first name and middle initial	Donor's last name	Donor's social security number

Address (number and street)	Legal residence (domicile)

City, State, and ZIP code	Citizenship

Did you file any gift tax returns for prior periods?. . . . . ☐ Yes ☐ No

If "Yes," state when and where earlier returns were filed ▶ ....

Name of consenting spouse	Consenting spouse's social security number

List of Gifts

Donee's name and address and description of gift (a)	Donor's adjusted basis of gift (b)	Date of gift (c)	Value at date of gift (d)

Consent

I consent to have the gifts made by my spouse to third parties during the calendar year considered as made one-half by each of us.

Consenting spouse's signature ▶ _____ Date ▶ _____

Under penalties of perjury, I declare that I have examined this return, and to the best of my knowledge and belief it is true, correct, and complete. Declaration of preparer (other than donor) is based on all information of which preparer has any knowledge.

Donor's signature ▶ .... Date ▶ ....

Preparer's signature
(other than donor's) ▶ .... Date ▶ ....

Preparer's address
(other than donor's) ▶ ....

For Paperwork Reduction Act Notice, see the instructions on the reverse of this form.   363–458–1   Form **709–A** (Rev. 7–82)

Form **709**	**United States Gift Tax Return**			OMB No. 1545-0020

Form **709**
(Rev. November 1983)
Department of the Treasury
Internal Revenue Service

United States Gift Tax Return
(Section 6019 of the Internal Revenue Code) (For gifts made after December 31, 1981 and before January 1, 1985)
Calendar year 19 _____.
▶ **For "Privacy Act" Notice, see the Instructions for Form 1040.**

OMB No. 1545-0020

Donor's first name and middle initial	Donor's last name	Social security number		
Address (number and street)		Domicile		
City, State, and ZIP code		Citizenship	**Yes**	**No**

If the donor died during the year, check here ▶ ☐ and enter date of death _____ , 19 _____.
If you received an extension of time to file this Form 709, check here ▶ ☐ and attach the Form 4868, 2688, 2350 or extension letter.
If you (the donor) filed a previous Form 709 (or 709-A), has your address changed since the last Form 709 (or 709-A) was filed? . . .

A Gifts by husband or wife to third parties.—Do you consent to have the gifts made by you and by your spouse to third
parties during the calendar year considered as made one-half by each of you? (See instructions.) . . . .
*(If the answer is "Yes," the following information must be furnished and your spouse is to sign the consent shown below.
If the answer is "No," skip lines 1-5 and go to Schedule A.)*

1(a) Name of consenting spouse	**1(b)** Social security number

2 Were you married to one another during the entire calendar year? (see instructions) . . . .

3 If the answer to 2 is "No," check whether ☐ married ☐ divorced or ☐ widowed, and give date (see instructions) ▶
4 Will a gift tax return for this calendar year be filed by your spouse? . . . .
5 **Consent of Spouse**—I consent to have the gifts made by me and by my spouse to third parties during the calendar year considered as made one-half by each of us. We are both aware of the joint and several liability for tax created by the execution of this consent.

Consenting spouse's signature ▶   Date ▶

Tax Computation	**1**	Enter the amount from Schedule A, line 13	**1**
	2	Enter the amount from Schedule B, line 3	**2**
	3	Total taxable gifts (add lines 1 and 2)	**3**
	4	Tax computed on amount on line 3 (see Table A in separate instructions)	**4**
	5	Tax computed on amount on line 2 (see Table A in separate instructions)	**5**
	6	Balance (subtract line 5 from line 4)	**6**
	7	Enter the unified credit from Table B (see instructions)	**7**
	8	Enter the unified credit against tax allowable for all prior periods (from Sch. B, line 1, col. (c))	**8**
	9	Balance (subtract amount on line 8 from amount on line 7)	**9**
	10	Enter 20% of the amount allowed as specific exemption after September 8, 1976 and before January 1, 1977 (see instructions)	**10**
	11	Balance (subtract line 10 from line 9)	**11**
	12	Unified credit (enter the smaller of line 6 or line 11)	**12**
	13	Credit for foreign gift taxes (see instructions)	**13**
	14	Total (add lines 12 and 13)	**14**
	15	Balance (subtract line 14 from line 6) (do not enter less than zero)	**15**
	16	Gift taxes prepaid with extension of time to file	**16**
	17	If line 16 is less than line 15, enter BALANCE DUE (see instructions)	**17**
	18	If line 16 is greater than line 15, enter AMOUNT TO BE REFUNDED	**18**

Please attach the necessary supplemental documents; see instructions.

Under penalties of perjury, I declare that I have examined this return, including any accompanying schedules and statements, and to the best of my knowledge and belief it is true, correct, and complete. Declaration of preparer (other than donor) is based on all information of which preparer has any knowledge.

Donor's signature ▶   Date ▶

Preparer's signature
(other than donor) ▶   Date ▶

Preparer's address
(other than donor) ▶

Please attach check or money order here

For Paperwork Reduction Act Notice, see page 1 of the separate instructions to this form.   Form **709** (Rev. 11-83)

SCHEDULE A.— Computation of Taxable Gifts (Gifts less medical and educational exclusions—see instructions)

Item number	Donee's name and address and description of gift. If the gift was made by means of a trust, enter trust's identifying number below and attach a copy of the trust instrument. If the gift was securities, enter the CUSIP number(s), if available.	Donor's adjusted basis of gift	Date of gift	Value at date of gift
1				

1	Total gifts of donor (see instructions)	1	
2	One-half of items _____ attributable to spouse (see instructions)	2	
3	Balance (subtract line 2 from line 1)	3	
4	Gifts of spouse to be included (from line 2 of spouse's return—see instructions)	4	
5	Total gifts (add lines 3 and 4)	5	
6	Total annual exclusions for gifts listed on Schedule A (including line 4) (see instructions)	6	
7	Total included amount of gifts, subtract line 6 from line 5	7	

Deductions (see instructions)

8	Gifts of interests to spouse for which a marital deduction will be claimed, based on items _____ of Schedule A	8		
9	Exclusions attributable to gifts on line 8	9		
10	Marital deduction—subtract line 9 from line 8	10		
11	Charitable deduction, based on items _____ to _____ less exclusions	11		
12	Total deductions—add lines 10 and 11		12	
13	Taxable gifts (subtract line 12 from line 7)		13	

Terminable Interest Marital Deduction. (see instructions)

☐ ◄ Check here if you elected, under the rules of section 2523(f), to include gifts of qualified terminable interest property on line 8, above. Enter the item numbers (from Schedule A, above) of the gifts for which you made this election _____

SCHEDULE B.— Did you (the donor) file gift tax returns for prior periods? (If "Yes," see instructions for completing Schedule B below.) ☐ Yes ☐ No

(a) Calendar year or calendar quarter (see instructions)	(b) Internal Revenue office where prior return was filed	(c) Amount of unified credit against gift tax for periods after December 31, 1976	(d) Amount of specific exemption for prior periods ending before January 1, 1977	(e) Amount of taxable gifts

1	Totals for prior periods (without adjustment for reduced specific exemption)	1	
2	Amount, if any, by which total specific exemption, line 1, column (d), is more than $30,000	2	
3	Total amount of taxable gifts for prior periods (add amount, column (e), line 1, and amount, if any, on line 2)	3	

(If more space is needed, attach additional sheets of same size.) ☐ U.S. GOVERNMENT PRINTING OFFICE: 1984- 421-108/253

APPENDIX 6

One doctor's will

Following is the text of a will disposing of the moderate-sized estate of a married physician, "Robert Aaron Miller," with two minor children. In order to eliminate, or at least minimize, the taxes on Mrs. Miller's estate if she outlives the doctor, his will sets up a bypass trust for the children, but leaves the income from it to his wife, who has no significant assets of her own. She also gets the rest of the estate, except for a bequest to the doctor's sister.

This text is presented solely to illustrate what such a will might contain. It has been simplified somewhat to make it easier for the nonlawyer to follow. For that reason, and because your will's wording must comply with the law and usage in your state to fulfill your intentions, the text should not be taken as your own model in substance or form.

Will of Robert Aaron Miller

I, Robert Aaron Miller, of 3240 Elm Road, Lakeview, in the County of Blank, State of Blank, do hereby make, publish, and declare this to be my Will.

1. As used in this Will:

(a) The word "give" shall, where applicable, be deemed to include "devise" and/or bequeath," and the word "pay" shall, where applicable, mean "convey, transfer, and pay."

(b) The words "my residuary estate" shall mean "all the rest, residue, and remainder of my estate and property, of whatever kind or nature and wherever situated."

(c) The words "in trust" shall mean "in trust, nevertheless, to hold, manage, control, invest and reinvest, and, until payment thereof as hereinafter directed, to receive the income thereof."

(d) The words "this Will" and words of reference to this Will shall be deemed to include any and all codicils hereto executed by me hereafter.

(e) The words "the Code" shall mean and refer to "the Internal Revenue

Code of 1954, as amended or replaced from time to time."

(f) The words "my wife" shall mean and refer to my wife, Jane.

2. I direct my Executor to pay my funeral expenses and my final medical expenses as expenses of my estate.

3. I give my wife, if she survives me, all my tangible personal property. If she does not survive me, my children who survive me shall divide such property among themselves by mutual agreement. Articles not so disposed of shall be sold by my Executor and the proceeds added to my residuary estate.

4. I give my wife, if she survives me, all of my right, title, and interest in any and all houses, condominiums, and/or cooperative apartments occupied by us as residences on a full- or part-time basis, including, as to any cooperative apartment, the corporate stock relating thereto.

5. If my wife does not survive me, I authorize and empower my Trustee, in his discretion, to retain any such residence or residences and any of my tangible personal property located therein as part of the principal of my children's trust for such period as the Trustee may deem advisable while such trust continues; to maintain such residence as a home for the benefit of any child or children of mine and their Guardians of the person, or any adult designated by such Guardians, without requiring them to pay rent; and to pay such charges for maintaining the residence from trust income or principal as the Trustee, in his discretion, shall determine.

6. I give my sister, Emily, if she survives me, the sum of $25,000 subject to the death tax directions in Paragraph 17. If she does not survive me, this gift shall lapse and be added to my residuary estate.

7. I give to my Trustee, to hold in trust as hereinafter provided, the largest amount that, by reason of the allowable unified credit and state death tax credit, will not cause federal estate tax to be payable.[A] The Executor may select cash or other estate assets, or both, to satisfy this provision.

8. I give my residuary estate to my wife if she survives me. If she does not, I give my residuary estate to my Trustee, to hold in trust under the provisions of Paragraph 13.

9. Notwithstanding anything in this will to the contrary, any power, duty, or discretionary authority granted to my Executor or my Trustee hereunder (other than the power to make elections permitted under any tax laws) shall be absolutely void to the extent that the right to exercise such power, duty, or authority, or the exercise thereof, shall in any way jeopardize or cause the disallowance to my estate of all or any part of the tax benefit afforded by the marital deduction provisions of the Code.

10. So long as my wife shall live, my Trustee shall pay to her or apply for her benefit all of the net income of the trust, at least annually, and may at any time pay to her or apply for her benefit such part of the principal of the trust as he shall in his discretion determine, without regard to my wife's other resources and without regard to the interest of any other person in the trust.[B]

11. My wife shall have the right to withdraw from principal such

amounts as she may request in writing from any Trustee (other than herself), but the total so withdrawn in any calendar year shall not exceed the greater of $5,000 or 5 percent of the fair market value of the trust determined as of the end of that year. This right of withdrawal shall be noncumulative.

12. My wife shall have the right to direct the Trustee to convert any non-income-producing trust property to income-producing property, and the Trustee shall comply within a reasonable time.

13. After the death of my wife, the remaining trust estate shall continue to be held by my Trustee in trust until my youngest surviving child attains the age of 25. Until then, any Trustee, in his discretion, may allot any part or all of the net income, in equal or unequal amounts, to one or more of the permissible beneficiaries. The permissible beneficiaries shall include my living children and the descendants of my deceased children. Any trust income not so allotted shall be added to principal.

14. When my youngest surviving child reaches the age of 25, the Trustee shall divide the remaining trust estate into as many equal shares as there are children of mine then living and children of mine then deceased with descendants then living. One share shall be paid to each such living child and one share to the descendants of each such deceased child.

15. The Trustee, in his discretion, may from time to time make preliminary distributions to any of my children who have attained the age of 25, if the remaining principal and income will be adequate for the health, support, maintenance, and education of my other children. The Trustee shall deduct such preliminary distributions without interest from the share ultimately distributed to each child or to each child's descendants.

16. If my wife disclaims any part (or all) of a gift under this will, I give what she disclaims to my Trustee to be added to the principal of the trust. The income from the disclaimed portion shall be added to my wife's other income from the trust.

17. I direct that all death taxes imposed on property included in my gross estate be paid out of my general estate as an administration expense.

18. I nominate my wife, Jane, as Executor under this will and my brother, Arthur, as Trustee and successor Executor. If he shall fail or cease to act, I name the First State Bank and Trust Company of Lakeview as Trustee and successor Executor. I request that no bond be required of any Executor or Trustee named herein.

19. If any minor child or children survive both my wife and me, I nominate as Guardian of the person of such child or children my sister, Emily, and as her successor my wife's borther, William H. Dawes. I nominate as Guardian of the property of such child or children my brother, Arthur, and as his successor my friend, James R. Bolton. I request that no bond be required of any Guardian named herein.

20. My wife alone during her lifetime may remove my Trustee and appoint a successor Trustee. After her death, the oldest adult trust benefi-

ciary—or if the oldest beneficiary is a minor, the Guardian of the property—shall have this power. This paragraph shall also apply if a Trustee resigns or ceases to act.

21. The Trustee may pay himself reasonable compensation from the trust estate during each calendar year for all ordinary services and reasonable additional compensation for any extraordinary services, all without court order. If the Trustee shall serve for a part of a calendar year, the annual compensation shall be prorated.

22. The Trustee may employ custodians, attorneys, accountants, investment advisers, or any other agents or advisers to assist him in the administration of the trust. The Trustee shall pay reasonable compensation to such agents or advisers from trust income or principal. These payments shall not decrease the compensation to which the Trustee is entitled.

23. In the administration of my estate, my Fiduciaries (Executor and Trustee) shall have all the powers now or hereafter conferred by law and may exercise any or all of those powers without court supervision unless required by law. In addition to and in amplification of the foregoing, I authorize my Fiduciaries to:

(a) Retain, abandon, sell (for cash or notes), lease, exchange, convey, divide, improve, or repair any estate property received or acquired;

(b) Invest and reinvest the trust estate in such securities, property, and other investments as men of prudence, discretion, and intelligence acquire for their own accounts;

(c) Borrow money from any person, firm, or corporation to meet any charges against my estate or for any other purpose relating to its administration, preservation, or enhancement, and to pledge or mortgage estate assets in connection with such borrowing; and

(d) Lend money to or purchase assets from the estate or a beneficiary thereof.

In witness whereof, I have to this, my Will, subscribed my name as of this date.

[A] This could channel some $600,000 of the doctor's estate into the trust, possibly leaving his wife less than he would prefer her to have outright. He could instead specify a nominal dollar amount here and allow her to determine how much more to add to the trust at his death via a disclaimer (see Paragraph 16).

[B] If the wife is named Trustee, her right to apply principal for her own benefit must be limited to the amount needed for her health, education, maintenance, and support in accordance with her accustomed standard of living; without this limitation, the trust principal may be taxable as part of her estate.

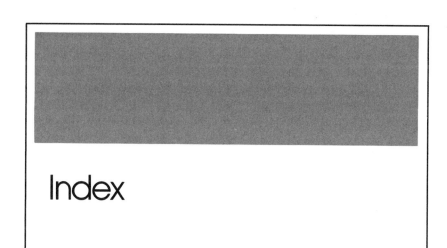

Index

retirement-plan life insurance, 71-72

tax sheltered, 2

worksheet for estimating, 76-77

See also Retirement planning

Per capita distribution, 23

Personal property

letter of instruction for, 47-48

sentimental bequests, 26

Per stirpes distribution, 23

Policy riders, 57

Portable pension funds, 96

Postretirement life insurance, 98

See also Life insurance

Practice management consultants, 144-145

Premarital agreements, 31

Private annuities, 120-122

Probate estate, 36-37

Profit-sharing plans, 68

Proof of competency, 32

Q

Q-TIP (Qualified Terminable-Interest Property) trust

federal estate taxes and, 12

pension funds and, 75

previous marriage and, 31

wills and, 20

R

Real estate

divorce and, 135

estate planning and, 91-93

gifts, 120

investment potential, 89-93

joint ownership and, 38

retirement plan and, 90-91

single doctors and, 129-131

See also Houses

Recapitalization, 119-120

Record keeping

administrative needs and, 44-48

See also Patient records

Relatives

federal estate taxes and, 13-14

wills and, 23-24

Remainder interest

gifts, 122, 123, 125

present value tables of, 155-157

Retained earnings, 99-100

Retired Lives Reserves, 98

Retirement-plan life insurance, 71-72

Retirement planning

bonds and, 86-88

common stocks and, 81-83

corporate life insurance and, 98

death benefits of, 58

defined-benefit pension plans, 66-69

incorporation and, 94-96

real estate investment and, 90-91

See also Pension funds

S

Second marriages

contested wills and, 31

See also Divorce

Securities bequests, 25-26

Separation (marital), 30

Severance pay

corporate disability insurance, 99

corporate life insurance, 97-98

corporate pension funds, 96

practice closing, 111

Short-term trusts

gifts to children, 116-118

See also Trusts

Single doctors, 127-135

administrative fees and, 132

divorce and, 132-135

gifts and, 127-129

real estate and, 129-131

second estate taxes and, 131-132

See also Marital status

Social Security survivor benefits, 53, 56

Solo practice

preserving value of, 105-107

selling of, 106-107

Specific bequests, 24-27

art objects/valuables, 26-27

charities, 25

medical libraries, 26

securities, 25-26

sentimental bequests, 26

staff/employees, 25

Split-funded retirement plan, 71

See also Retirement planning

Spousal remainder trust

gifts to children, 118-119

See also Trusts